A Travel Through Time

Collaborative Works by Kids who made a
Difference at Lovin Elementary School - 2014

3G Publishing, Inc.
Loganville, Ga 30052
www.3gpublishinginc.com
Phone: 1-888-442-9637

First published by 3G Publishing, Inc. September, 2014

ISBN: 978-1-941247-05-1

Printed in the United States of America

CONTENTS

Dedication

You are sweet, funny, and just overall magnificent, I couldn't ask for a better teacher! ~ *Mariam Drammeh*

Thank you Ms.Argilagos for all that you do. My writing really improved this last year. ~ *Cooper Clickner*

To Ms. Argilagos, My writing teacher that opened my eyes and got me on this path of writing. ~ *Spencer Young*

Thank you, Mrs. Argilagos for distributing kindness, joy, creativity, and enthusiasm to the classroom in 5th grade and guiding us to a wonderful opportunity. ~ *John Greene*

Mrs. Argilagos really helped me to grow and express my feelings as a writer!" ~ *Alondra Gonzales*

Thank you Mrs. Argilagos for everything that you have done for us. From the little teaching points to the life changing habits you have helped us through not only our school year, but our life. I love you Mrs.Argilagos. ~ *Dalton Holland*

"I give great thanks to my Language Arts teacher Mrs. Argilagos. Thanks to her I have now improved my writing to a greater level. ~ *Chiderah Iheagwara*

Thanks for helping me get better in writing, and for giving us this opportunity! ~ *Jaiden O. Anderson*

Thank you Mrs.Argilagos for a hilarious year of ups and downs last year! ~ *Ava Leaphart*

We dedicate this book to Ms. Arigilagos, whose passion and dedication to her students, made this dream come true! ~ *Nakyla Brooks-Stallings*

Ms. Arigilagos, we dedicate this book to you, because you taught us to excel and never give up. You made us bring our thoughts to life in our writing. You also gave us an opportunity we never even dreamed of achieving at our age, becoming authors. Thank you Ms. Arigilagos, we will never forget you. We love you! ~ *YOUR ENTIRE CLASS*

Amil
Mohamed

CHAPTER 1

1781
Colin's Big Adventure

By: Amil Mohamed

My week has been tough. Nothing has been going well. I haven't seen my dad in what has seemed like ages. Now that I am thinking about him I'm starting to get worried. He's never been gone for this long. Mom said he was working late shifts at the blacksmith shop. In her eyes I could tell she was holding something back, but I couldn't tell what it was. That was when I really started to worry about my dad.

Weeks had gone by, and no one had seen my father. At nightfall I heard my mother crying and I decided to see what the matter was. That is when I felt my heart race a million miles per second. My dad was at war against the British. Messengers had been spreading rumors about how many people were killed during one battle. That was when our minister appeared at our step. He informed us that our father had been shot and was killed. This sudden event broke my heart into a million pieces that could never be put back together. This was the start of revenge. I was in a phase that could not be put to the side. I was going to find that man and demolish him.

That night while I was a sleep I had a horrific dream. I dreamt of my dad getting killed right before my eyes. It got worse; the British soldier was killing my dad right in front of my bare eyes. That was when I decided to do something about this event. As the night continued I packed my stuff in a knapsack and went off into the night like a burglar seeking revenge.

As the night sky became bright and brighter I gotten deeper into the dark and mushy grounds of the battlefields. As I was running through the battle fields something caught my attention. It was all the dead body's laying around the battlefields. There I saw it lying there hopelessly was a kid's body. The thought I was having while running was who would do this type of horrific thing. This thought almost made me turn around. The only thing that stopped was my commitment to finding my father.

Although I have been trudging through these mucky, bloody fields for two hours it seems like two days. I wasn't really walking with a reason but with a purpose. Then all of a sudden I was nearly feet away from a raging battle... the battle of Yorktown. I knew I would just dead if I wound up like my father dead if I go looking for him in a raging battle. Then a solider in red appeared out of nowhere and shot me dead center in the chest. As seconds went by they seemed like hours. I had blacked out the second the bullet blood so I really didn't remember if there was blood coming out. Only one thing benefited out of being shot was that I got to be with my dad in heaven.

As I started to gain my conscious back, I noticed that I wasn't on the ground anymore. I was in some tent thing on a cot. It was some type of infirmary that treated the people wounded in war. The doctor gave me medication so my pain would subside. Then all of a sudden a man in old uniform rushed in and hugged me. It had seemed like that hugged knocked some sense into me because I started me over remembering who I was. Then the most joy came over me. That strange man wasn't so strange anymore. That man was my dad! It had seemed like God had granted me some magical wish. I had become the happiest boy in the world!

CHAPTER 2

1839
Time for a Break, a Freedom Break

By: Jaiden Anderson

In 1839 a miracle was made in Brooklyn, New York at the Brooklyn hospital. A baby named Kodi Brown was born. He had the biggest smile you could ever see and perhaps the happiest baby you will ever see. But what if this smile turned upside down, and turned into a great big frown? Yes, I said it Kodi's smile was about to go *poof*. The reason I say this is because Kodi's parents were runaways. This means they were slaves, and they ran away from their plantation. Kodi found this out later down the happy/sad trail he walks in his life. This is the story of Kodi Brown.

Smiles, frowns, and tears passed and Kodi had met some friends in the past 12 years he has been alive. His best friend out of all would be Timothy Wayne. Boy they were the best of friends! They told each other secrets, they had play dates, and the number one rule of being somebody's best friend is to share your food with them no matter what the circumstance. Timothy invited Kodi and his parents to his house for dinner. "Ding-Dong." Kodi and his parents have arrived to the Wayne residence. When the door opened a huge cloud of smoke knocked them out, but wasn't strong enough to kill them. In what felt like a heartbeat, they awoke in a dark chamber surrounded by other African Americans.

"Wake up my little children it's time to start the auction." The voice sounded like a deep, but light voice. Kodi looked up and saw nothing until the big door opened. He saw what looked like Timothy, but taller. He walked out the door and saw lots of white men willing to bid on slaves. Kodi thought this was a dream, but when he tried to get out the dreamscape, he couldn't. Hours later, he was the only one left to bid on, so he was sold to Timothy's dad, Tim Wayne. Crazy, huh? His best friend set him up and lured him into a trap.

Later that summer, Kodi was picking cotton for Master Wayne, but he wasn't doing a good job. Another kid like him glanced at him with a friendly look. The kid walked over and introduced himself. "Hi I'm Cesar but people around here call me "The Crazy One" because I know all about the Underground Railroad". Kodi was shocked because he thought that was a myth and it would never in a million years be true. Cesar said he was leaving today at midnight. Kodi doubted him.

The next day Kodi walked to go get some breakfast. He saw Cesar getting beat before his own eyes, and it made him want to break FAST. He ran and ran and ran. He hardly saw Cesar anymore, but when he did, he told Kodi that he was beat for digging for the Underground Railroad.

Years and years passed, but to Kodi it felt like decades. Kodi knew how to shovel because he did it for nearly 4 years now. He was 16 years of age and had no way to get out of that plantation like his parents did. He looked up from shoveling and saw a young woman trudging through the snow. Kodi knew this lady. It was Gertie Davis. She always talked nonsense since the first day they met. But when she said "my mom is Harriet Tubman," it was hard not to listen.

After Gertie explained her story, Kodi found out they have a lot in common. For once he found someone that has been through something like him. She was also lured into a trap. Her mother was using the Underground Railroad to help her daughter escape. She invited Kodi to come with them, and he agreed to the plan. So they waited, and waited, and waited until they were getting too old to wait. They were now old enough to buy a house and even marry each other, but, they had a surprise that night.

BUMP, THUMP, and more BUMPS!! Kodi had a bad dream, but the thumps and bumps weren't just in his dream. He looked up, saw the door crack open, and he got that feeling he had the day he saw Cesar getting beat. The moon gazed a silhouette around two figures holding hand and hand. They came closer and he saw Gertie and Harriet Tubman. It was happening! They left as quickly as a shadow and ran like three cheetahs being chased by a killer!

They traveled lightly with only food, water, and a few clothes. It was a long way to Brooklyn, but they could make it happen. It would take months. They constantly moved from house to house swiftly and stealthily. To Kodi, only one week would feel like months, and he was anxious to get to Brooklyn. He has been waiting for this for years, but they can't back down or walk away They've come too far!

After more of what felt like years they arrived at what looked like the last house like no other. It blinked its beautiful lights. Someone knocked on the door, and knocked on the door, and knocked on the door a few more times. Harriet understood the code which said "This is your last stop travelers and you need to hurry before you miss the train." They waited 3 months to get here and when sunrise peeked through the windows, they were home!

At the end, Kodi got a job, and he and Gertie were happily married. Everything came and went. Sadly, Kodi never heard from his parents since he was 12. The good thing was that Kodi and Gertie became old and died together in 1913. At least they managed to escape using the Underground Railroad, together!

Emily Jameson

CHAPTER 3

1848
The Town

By: Emily Jameson

A fat tear rolled down my cheek as I watched the red caboose of the train take my father to California. I never wanted this to happen. Why did this gold rush have to happen? Sure, I wanted my family to get rich, but only a cabbage head wouldn't. I toyed with my hair on the carriage ride home and frowned at all the buildings, people, and animals as we passed them. Jonah and Susan the horses, my two friends from school Caroline and Emma, and I glared at the train tracks that passed through our farm as if they had wronged me, or one of my friends. I glared at the small house on the Johnson Farm until I realized it was mine. I hopped off the carriage to walk into the house. I walked into my room to finish my homework. I scribbled the answers down at top speed and tried to read my own hand writing. I can, but barely. I hopped into bed and fell asleep.

The next day I ran downstairs like I do every Saturday and got the chicken eggs. I wrote on the paper on the wall that Dolly laid three, Molly laid two, and Holly laid two. I left one for each to raise, as a new chicken when it hatches. I then checked in my favorite chicken, Polly. She lays the most every time and had laid four. I took three and checked in our rooster, Jolly. He needed feeding so I grabbed the bag of corn and grain and spread it out on the ground and opened the chicken coop so all the chickens can eat. Then I went to get the mail.

I opened the box by the front door and found three things. The shoes mother bought for me and the box of ribbons for my hair came. And then came the letter. I brought it up to mother. She opened it and smiled. She looked at me and said "Were going to California. Start packing." I jumped up and ran to my room and grabbed my suitcase. I packed every outfit I owned and chose a dress to wear on the train. I set my weaving in a bag and set it in my suit case. Then I set my favorite trophies in the extra space. The golden pouch I won in a weaving contest. The silver bracelet I won in a painting contest. I set them down care-fully on a thin layer of soft feathers. I closed the suitcase and walked downstairs.

I took one last look at my house as I hopped into the train. It looked smaller from here, but it was still the same house. My violet eyes darted around to take in one last look at the town. It looked whole new place now that I was leaving it. I turned towards mother and saw that she was feeling the same. I grabbed her hand and pulled her into the train.

The train was roomy and had comfy seats. It had a cart for eating, one for sleeping, and one to sit around in. I yawned and went to claim two beds for mother and I while mother went to get food. I threw mothers bag on a bottom bunk and claimed the top. I climbed on and dozed off. But soon I woke up to a loud bump! I was confused until mother came in looking scared and said "The train is being hijacked!"

I grabbed my bag and helped mother with hers and soon we were off the train and in a dusty town. We were the only ones who got off before it sped off. I turned around and saw a sign "The name of this town is Rode." I read aloud.

I picked up my suitcase and walked towards the town. I knew father sending us tickets was too good to be true. Immediately I started to fill with anger. I glared at everything with an infuriated glint in my eye. I saw everything as a reason to be even angrier. All the pain I went through starting from when father said he was going to go mine for gold just refused to stop going through my head. Why did it have to end up here? I hated this puny western town already.

A little boy who looked about six stared at me through the window. He had short brown hair. A girl about my age with the same color hair as the small boy walked to the window to see what he was looking at. I looked around and saw that many of the homes had a for sale sign in the front. I was about to tell mother when a large dog bounded up to us. I held out a hand for it to smell. It licked my hand and fell over to have a belly rub after mother let it sniff her hand. She smiled.

All of a sudden, people were streaming out of houses to welcome us. They were introducing themselves and mother introduced us to them. I found out that the boy who looked about six was named Jimmy and the girl who looked about my age was named Jenny. I decided to try to be friends with her I told mother and she said "Excellent choice, because her mother is my new best friend. She can sew and weave anything in a second, just like you said I can." I looked at mother and smiled.

The lady at the front desk of the building buyers place smiled as we walked in. Mother walked right up to her and said that we wanted to buy the house they call 03 Rider Street. I remembered that the house was tall and very wide. I remembered the room I would have as mine and smiled. Big and beautiful, it came with a large bed and a case of toys the last person who lived here outgrew. As soon as the paperwork was done, I grabbed mothers hand and half pulled half dragged her to the house.

I ran to my room and threw open thy toy chest. What a sight to see all those toys I have wanted for years! A large wooden top, a chess set, and a box of silk hair ribbons were what I saw first. I took them out to see what other wonders the chest held. I saw a large wooden box with no label. I opened it to find a pot of paint and a paint brush. I jumped up and ran to tell mother what I have found.

Mother was at the table writing a letter. I checked the name and address of the person she was writing to and discovered it was to father! I smiled and went to play with Jenny. We played in the small pond by her house until mother called me inside because it was time for supper. I smiled and gave Jenny four of the eight silk ribbons. She stared at them in awe and smiled. I ran to my house to eat supper, which was chicken and cactus juice. Then I went straight to bed, just as mother says I should.

I woke up the next morning and heard a banging at the door. It was a letter! I recognized the handwriting as my fathers. I excitedly ripped it open. Inside was a note saying that he had sold the farm and was coming to live with us. I jumped up and ran as fast as I can to show it to mother. She read it three times before she believed it. When she finished, she looked up and smiled at me. I ran to prepare a room for father.

I woke the next morning to yet another knock on the door and recognized the familiar pattern. I jumped up and ran to meet father.

Sidi Ndiaye

CHAPTER 4

1849
Road to Freedom

By: Sidi Ndiaye

Ahh! Ahh! As I work on planting corn a high pitched sound startles me. I turned and the sounds of a short African American lady caught the attention of my eye. The second I turned my eye the lady was being pounded with a stick. While all of that madness was happening, my eyes started to become blurry. Watching this woman being beaten was so miserable. I just wish I could do something about it. "Cameron Tubman, come here". A familiar voice calling my name makes its way into my eardrum. I knew the voice just not the person. The person who called my name kept repeating it over and over again. While my name was being called, I followed the path of where the voice was coming from.

As I walked anxiously through the pathway, butterflies filled my stomach. Tiny drops of sweat rolled from head to toe. The most negative thoughts piled up in my tiny brain. There was just one thought that stuck out the most. It was you were being sold from your master. I knew that was wrong though. I finally entered the room. It didn't take me a long time to figure out that the white guy, with a black wig, with a suit and tie was my master. I didn't know what to say. I literally squealed out loud. "Cameron you and your family are going to a slave sale", the master said. After that was announced the only sounds in that room was crying. I think the master started to chuckle.

As we ambled to the slave sale my entire family sobbed. I just couldn't believe it. We are actually never going to see each other again. As time passed by, slaves were being sold. Suddenly, the low pitched noise of my master was heard. He announced our last name. That meant we were about to be sold. While walking up the stairs onto the stage, my heart was pumping quicker than a cheetah. I bet everyone in my family felt the same way. These were the last seconds we would ever be together. Minutes passed by as we were being wagered with money. Finally, the wager was over. A man named Charles Deanlers had gotten us for $800. Shuffling towards my new owner, a noise stopped my feet.

It was the master! He exclaimed that not all of us were going to Mr. Charles, only one of us. That's when we started to get switched. Unfortunately, I had to stay with my old master. I sobbed the whole way back wondering when I would be able to meet my family again. By the time we got back to the master's house, the master put me in my crowded hut. People kept on asking me, how was it? I ignored them. I couldn't fall asleep, because I was just way too aggravated about the slave sale. Eventually, I fell asleep until I heard a noise that practically gave me a heart attack. All I could see was a woman shaped figure with a couple of people behind her. I was scared to death. I didn't know what to say. I was speechless. For a minute, we all just kept starring at each other. It was awkward. It was silent until the woman started to ask me questions. She asked me questions like, do you like slavery? I basically said no to every   question.

The question was, do you want to escape slavery? I said yes. That was the hardest decision I had ever made in my life. What if I got caught? How hard would my punishment be? After my uncertain decision we packed up our insignificant amount of clothes and took off. Since we lived in Georgia and our goal was Pennsylvania, it would take a long time, but I was ready for the job.

For our safety, we climbed from tree to tree while slave catchers were not watching us. Around 1:00 in the morning we all started to get exhausted, so we decided to stop by a house that had the most unusual sign in the world. The woman said that the sign meant it was okay for us to sleep there for the night. I was relieved that we got to stay at someone's house that actually cared about us, unlike the master. As soon as I got into that house, I was so drowsy that as soon as I got in that house I fell asleep right away. Let me be the first to say that I just had the best sleep in ages.

We had to leave really early though, which stunk. When we left Tennessee at 4:00 in the morning, the woman told us there were no more stops we were going to take. We used our same strategy the rest of the trail. I kept on getting tired, but I had enough perseverance to keep going. Day by day, night by night, it was a bitter struggle. It took at least one week and six days with no stops. Then, I saw a pretty sun rise. That was the day we would be free, I knew it would be. Finally, I saw the fresh light.

That was the light that would guide me to freedom. I took one more step, and I was in Pennsylvania. The joy filled up inside of me. Just knowing that I was finally free was the best feeling in the world. I screamed with joy. I would like to see the master's face now. As content as I was, there still was a gloomy part in me. Knowing that I was in freedom and the rest of my family didn't get to enjoy this experience with me was miserable. Suddenly I heard this voice that caught my eardrum's attention. Once again the person was repeatedly calling my name. I turned over to look, and I couldn't believe who it was.

It was my mom! Harriet Tubman. It turns out she was the one guiding me to freedom. I couldn't believe it was her this entire time. We both started to dance. I know that the rest of my family isn't here, but at least I'm with my mom. My mom and I spent the rest of the day trying to find someone willing enough to let us stay there until we got on our feet. We finally found someone. The person was the same woman who let us stay at her house during the trip. She said that she had moved, because she didn't like the environment in Tennessee. We rested at her home for the rest of the day. Then, it was time to go to bed. I couldn't fall asleep because of a noise. Later on I figured out what that noise was. It wasn't a pretty seen when I figured it out.

While I was trying to fall asleep, sounds of boots woke me up. I was trying to ignore the noise, but it was way too loud. Suddenly, my door opened. I didn't move or breathe. I figured out that it was a slave catcher!!!! The slave catcher just took a quick glance and never noticed me. He just left the house after he inspected my room. The rest of the night I had the worst nightmares, but I knew they would go away. In the morning I told my mom about them, and she said it was going to be just fine.

I believed her and knew it was going to be just fine. I will always remember the trip I took with my mom to the Road of Freedom. Remember, SLAVERY IS WRONG!!!!!

Dalton Holland (signature)

CHAPTER 5

1850
Those Who Seek Freedom

By: Dalton Holland

"Noooooooo! Don't do it!" I demanded. And there I was. In a puddle of my own father's blood. Drowning in depths of fear, thinking about life without him. They had just treated him like a rag-doll, and now they were sending me to America to do the same thing to me.

Person by person they started loading us onto the ships. They acted like there wasn't a care in the world. Little did they know they just killed the apple of my eye, the light of my life. They didn't give him a well-deserved funeral, a swift stab to the heart and just like that, my heart was crushed. Although I had just seen a catastrophic event, they expected me to drag my broken heart to America and start working for some lazy whites. They had intended the wrong thing.

We finally arrived. The tears in the past where still in my

mind, but I knew I had to work hard if I wanted to survive. They dropped us of at Mr. Thomas' plantation and left us to rot in our own misery. Mr. Thomas nicely introduced himself, but then it started. He was like an eagle, waiting for us to make a fatal mistake. His whip was always at the spot, waiting to bring misery and destruction to the aching bones of me and the other captives. I and my family knew we couldn't live like this, so we made a crucial decision.

It was a pitch black night. We were silently walking through the dense dark forest. My mom Yolanda led the group with me and the middle. My brother Shawn followed behind me,   with my father Martin looking down at us from heaven. Martin gave us courage, luck, and determination to escape the cruel world we were living in. We had made it for a while. We were confident we could make it to the North, but then there was a sound. We saw a tall figure running at us like we had just his family. "RUN!" I franticly shouted out. Then we were off to the races. I peered over my shoulder to see a white figure running at us! "Slave Hunters!" I thought. But it was too little too late.

The person whipped us and told us we better pray if we wanted to stay alive. He treated us with no sympathy. He was hauling us around like dogs on a leash. We didn't know where he was taking us. Unanswered questions were ringing in our frightened minds, "Would we be separated, or will they even keep us alive!" Will they keep us alive is the kind of question you never want to ask, and it makes me cringe thinking about losing another family member.

"Don't leave us!" I screamed. The tall man brutally whipped us until my mom and I were unconscious. I woke up several hours later in an empty room; the aftermath of the whipping was still fresh in my mind and body. "I'm so tired of this!" I think to myself. What if we treated them how they

30

treated us? What if we inflicted harm on them because of their skin color? I don't think they would like it if we treated them like this, because we don't!

Several moments later a short white man in handsome clothes approached us and shouted, Get out here and work you Negroes! Now a terrible thought arises in my mind. "Please don't say we are at a different plantation!" I desperately say in my mind. The unfamiliar person whips the doors open, I blink, then there I am standing in a field of pain, misery, despair, and some blood every once in a while. No progress was made; I was back working for some lazy Whites, without my brother there to help me through tough moments. A few days had passed without getting whipped. Our new slave owner had a name for me. He called me 'Trouble Maker.' This new slave owner was even tougher than Mr. Thomas. A girl got caught trying to read and he ended up whipping her so bad that she couldn't work for 3 weeks! We knew it would be hard to escape, and if we got caught we would never come back, but we were willing to do anything to get away from this crazy place.

"It's time." My mom whispers to me. There were butterflies in my empty stomach as we started our trek into the lonely forest. This time we had a plan, we were going to stop at some place called the Underground Railroad and stay the night. We would then make our way up North to where African Americans were treated how they were supposed to be treated, like human beings.

We started out by running as far away as we could for safety. After a few hours, my empty stomach and miss-treated body started to take over. I sat down on a rugged rock and then it came out. I threw up as my mom rubbed my back. "We are almost there sweetie pie, don't give up" My mom exclaimed in a courageous voice. Her voice gave me a burst of confidence. I then sprung up and continued my journey.

"I see light!" I screamed. We ran to the house that has the candle lit and knocked on the door. A quick 'whoosh' as the door swung open and there I was standing in front of a face I thought I would never see again, Shawn!

Hugs were shared as we all asked the same question, "HOW!" He told us he was taken to another plantation, where he escaped to the Underground Railroad. Instead of going up North, he wanted to help all the people like him, trying to leave and go to where they really belong, in a free place. We were amazed at the decision Shawn made. He put his life on the line every day to help people like him. "That's my boy!" My mom said to Shawn in glee. We went to sleep that night blessed that we had found our love.

"I'm ready to go up to the North!" I said in an exciting tone. Little did I know Shawn and Yolanda weren't so ready. They stalled then they finally made a proposal that would change my life. "We need to stay and help all the fugitives." Shawn stated. We agreed that it was the only right thing to do. Now I'm here, doing what I've always wanted to do, not to escape to the North, but to help those who seek freedom.

Hana Burns

CHAPTER 6

1850
Cold and Cruel

By: Hana Burns

My hands start to tremble and I start to shake. "Who wants this raggedy woman for let's say... Fifteen dollars?" Mr. Kenlin said to the other slave owners. "No! Not mama!"" I scream in my head. "Okay! Seems like an awesome deal!" Another slave owner says. I saw mama stare at me in tears as she walked away. My face started to turn red and I wanted to scream at all the slave owners. But, what could I do? I'm just another worthless slave to all the others. My tears couldn't stop running down my face and I couldn't stop shaking in rage. I watch mama as she takes her steps to who knows where. While her body gets smaller and smaller as she walks in the distance, my heart beats faster and faster. Mama is gone.

The sun sets and it gets colder. While the slaves and I walk to our working field, I remember what had happened earlier today. Mr. Kenlin finally says, "Okay, go to bed everyone!" Everyone puts their shovels down and sighs with relief. We walk to our "beds" and go to sleep. At night, I slept alone. While I tried to go to sleep, I prayed that mama was okay. "I miss mama... a lot." I tell myself. A tear rolls down my face again. "Why?" I ask myself, "Why?" I try hard to get myself to sleep, and I eventually do.

The next morning, I woke up by the loud bang of pots, pans, and the blow of a horn. I rub my eyes, and put my long, black hair in a bun. "Ugh, here we go again." I whisper in my head. Mr. Kenlin walks up to me and says, "Enna, today I want you to work in the daisy field and pick daisies. I will tell you when to work with the dirt bags again." "Yes, sir." I say while nodding my head. I walk out into the yellow blazing sun, beginning to rise. I walk all the way to the daisy garden with my basket and sit down. I pick a flower and look at it. "How beautiful," I say. Daisies were mama's favorite. "These daisies are beautiful, but not as beautiful as you." Mama would say.

"I really hope mama is okay." I say while picking more flowers. "If mama's okay, then I'm okay." I pick flowers for so long that my arm gets tired and my hands start to hurt. "How many flowers do they need?" I ask myself. After about a couple minutes later, I see Mr. Kenlin walking towards me. "Okay, you need to work with the dirt bags, now." Mr. Kenlin tells me. "Yes, sir," I say again. I handed him the basket and he took it inside. I walked all the way to where the dirt and the bags were. I picked up my shovel and started to dig the dirt, and put it in the bags. The sun was beaming down onto my face, and boy, it was HOT. I wiped the sweat off my forehead. After about an hour of scooping dirt and putting them into bags, I had to stop and catch my breath for a moment. When I stood back up, someone tapped me on the shoulder.

"Yes, Mr. Kenlin?" I said without turning around. "It's not Mr. Kenlin." A familiar voice said behind me. I froze. I closed my eyes and there again my heart started to beat faster and faster just like when mama was leaving. "It can't be." I say. I turn around and there she is. The person that made me feel like I was more than a slave and thought I was more beautiful than a daisy was standing right in front of me. "Mama," I gasped. "Mama!" I put my shovel down and I jumped into her arms. "I can't believe you're here!" I tell mama. "Me, either!" she says. My eyes start to water and I sniffle.

Mama puts me down and wipes my eyes with the back of her hand. "Don't cry. I'm here now," she says. "Now, let's get you and me working, so we don't get in trouble." "Okay." I pick my shovel back up, and she opens the bag. I shovel the dirt up and put it in the bag. While I did that, I flashed mama a smile, and she smiled back. "I love you, mama." I say to her. "I love you too, honey."

CHAPTER 7

1856
Saving Azi

By: Kimberly Roberts

Dear Journal, I am the oldest from 4 sisters and 3 brothers. Which is 7 total. I have a mom and a dad except they are all gone now. I just wish I had a chance to say bye to them before they left me. It all began when slavery began for my family in 1856. When we had heard the news about slavery spreading and people being sent to work on plantations, my mama quickly decided we needed to move to a free state. My mama had already bought a house and everything. I was only 5 so I didn't really understand what was going on. We were going to leave on Saturday, and it was Wednesday. We received a knock at the door, and quickly I knew it was something terrible by the look on mama's face.

We were sent to a master named Patrick Henry who had 56 laves before us and 65 after. When we got to his plantation right away he was harsh, but is daughter named Lizzie was very sweet. I started working inside cleaning rooms and helping prepare dinner, but I didn't clean Lizzie's room. When I was supposed to be cleaning her room, she would secretly teach me how to read and write, so one day I can escape. Even though slaves aren't allowed to lean to read or write. They were our little secretes, but then everything changed. Lizzie's dad found out what we were doing and whooped us both, but didn't tell anybody about me learning how to read.

I had to start working on the fields, and right away it was terrible! I had to pick cotton by hand because back then slaves weren't allowed to use machines because they didn't have any. At the end of the day my hands would ache like crazy. They would have red bumps and white puss would come out of them. I would also have many bruises from the thorns of the bushes, and my hands hurt so much that I couldn't even carry my basket. I was little and I didn't understand why us black kids had to work on the fields while white kids got to have fun at school. And the worst part was that we worked for those kids who got to be lazy the whole day. Why couldn't we go to school?

I only had my brother and my sister left .Azi and Caleb. Plus my parents, but mama keeps saying that Caleb is going to be sold soon. I asked Lizzie, but she only told me that he was going to go away for a while. I guess it was too sad for her to tell me. I didn't want my sister or me have to see my brother go away. Especially Azi since she was only 6. I had to go talk to him, but it was too late. When I got to his room he was already on the stage and the caller was calling numbers.

Mama said that she wanted to leave slavery before anybody else from our family could be sold. She said we would leave the next day with a nice lady named Harriet Tubman.

She would help slaves escape slavery and live in a free state. It was a very dark night when all the masters were asleep. We crept through the darkening woods until it got so dark that we had to use lanterns. We began seeing a distant body of Water where we would find a boat to sail away. Before we reached the boat I turned back to tell my parents, but they weren't there. I searched and searched for them, but I couldn't find them. Just then...... AHHHH OH MY GOS!!!!!!!!

My parents were dead right in front of my bare eyes that were just aching to cry. I pulled Azi behind a tree to hide.

" Hey what should we do with them?" said a darkening voice appearing to come closer and closer.

"I don't know but I do know that father is not going to like some dead slaves." Said the other man

"Your right let's leave them here, and go."

"What happen...?" Azi asked

"Nothing Shhh." I whispered back

From that point on I vowed to keep Azi always by my side, since she was the only one I had left. We left without saying another word and we did manage to get to the boat safely without getting caught. We had about a 6 hour trip before Mrs. Harriet Tubman said to get off. We got to the area that she left us in which was a small playground are with black kids playing. Then there was a room where everyone had their own bed. I remember Azi quickly run away the soon we got there. She went to play on the playground with some other kids her age. I sat down on a bench they had inside. I watched as Azi played and laughed with the other kids. I had wished I could have fun like her, but I had so much on my mind that I couldn't play at the moment.

I went to ask a lady where the restroom was, and I went. When I came out I heard everyone screaming and running to their mothers, but Azi didn't have anyone to run to. A very tall officer came into the room and just shot someone and left. He shot I little named Azi. I fell to my knees.

" NOOOO AZI!!!!!!" I yelled as he ran away and I ran to Azi. Nobody rushed to get help because they knew she wouldn't survive a shot to the head. I didn't get caught because for some reason they didn't have a file for a lost slave named Charlotte. I hadn't kept my promise to keep Azi safe, and I'm still mad at myself for that to this very day.

Spencer Young (handwritten signature)

CHAPTER 8

1912
The Sinking of the Titanic

By: Spencer Young

"Bonk, crash, bonk!" that was all John Henry could hear. He was in the middle of a scorching factory making pieces of the Titanic. In a different factory the inner anatomy was being constructed. It was June 22nd, 1908; the construction on the Titanic had just barely begun. John was asked to help build the Titanic because he works well under pressure, and is the only passenger allowed below decks.

It's April 10th, 1912; John was marveled at the immense size of the ship, and was so consumed in thought, he almost forgot to buy tickets! Suddenly he recalled, by orders from the captain that he got to go on for free! He ventured all over the massive ship before he entered his room. He was intrigued how well his room was prepared. He adored checking in places he hasn't checked before!

April 11th, 10:30p.m. John couldn't sleep, so he took a midnight stroll. (But it wasn't midnight.) When he was walking past the radio operator, he took a rest before continuing. He overheard the radio spurting ice berg warnings. The drowsy operator dozed off and John left him to snore in peace. John thought that no ice berg could sink the Titanic. He was on a floating palace! After that, John swiftly left back to his cabin and little did he know he was in grave danger.

April 12th, 8:35 P.M. John leapt out of his bed, jumbled on all of his clothes, and raced to the breakfast hall where a long awaited meal was waiting on a silver platter. (Literally!) He dodged multiple packs of ravenous and raging groups of children! He ate a luxurious breakfast and ate until he felt like he was going to burst! John took a long nap and snapped awake when he was shaken off his bed. When he came to his senses he saw a big chocolate colored dog on his bed! He wobbled as he raised himself of the floor; he wondered how the dog had gotten in. He looked around and saw that he had left the door open! He walked to the outside of the Titanic and sat down. He wondered why the air seemed so brisk.

April 13th 11:58 P.M. John was fast asleep when he felt a massive crash! He felt the engine stall and stop. And then the lights went out, so he stumbled and tripped in the dark. April 14th, John ran outside and stared at a gaping hole where water was gushing into the ship. He ran like a cheetah to get to the strike zone and he discovered that an ice berg had sliced through the side of the ship! He ran up to the cabin to warn the captain about the damage, but the captain was already informed. The captain was franticly sending crew-members everywhere to warn everyone and to get them safe!

April 15th, John was sprinting down the halls to get to the lifeboats, but he was halted by a crew-member keeping him from getting on a lifeboat. After the lifeboats were lowered, he knew that he had to help others survive. He helped as many as he could get off the ship. Suddenly the ship reared up! John tumbled and was knocked out by colliding with the railing. When he woke up he had a throbbing pain in his side and head, and he noticed that he was in the hospital. He couldn't remember what happened after he hit his head, but he knew that the sinking of the Titanic was a worldwide tragedy. He wouldn't forget that horrid day.

CHAPTER 9

1912
Surviving a Deadly Disaster

By: Chiderah Iheagwara

" Extra, extra, read all about the unsinkable ship Titanic!"
Madiline heard as she was writing her birthday list. It was
one more day till it was her birthday and she couldn't wait!
Madiline was on her way home before her mom got off
work. She wanted to show her mother her birthday wish
list hoping to get tickets for the Titanic.

When Madiline got home, she saw her mother in the
kitchen. "Look mother, I made my birthday list!" Madiline said as she was running in the kitchen. Her mother
looked up from the dirty dishes. She sighed as she read the
list. "Madiline my sweet pie, I can't afford this stuff," she
said. Madiline forced herself a smile as she walked away.
She soon let the tears flow down her rosy cheeks while she
was out of her mother's sight. She knew her family didn't
have a lot of money, but all she really wanted was tickets to

go on the titanic. Time had passed and Madiline finally fell asleep.

The sun slowly rose up in the aquamarine sky. Madiline slowly woke up as the sun shouted for her to get out of bed. Madiline rose up and trudged downstairs. As she was walking, Madiline noticed a note on the table. Madiline made a strange face. She walked over to the brown table and unfolded the note. Two pieces of vanilla paper fell out of the folded note. Her eyes suddenly widened as she picked up the two pieces of paper. She couldn't believe it. Suddenly the door opened. Madiline's mother walked inside and looked at Madiline with a smile on her face. "I see you found the tickets huh?" said Madiline's mother. Madiline's face shined as the stars in the midnight sky. She was so excited, she couldn't believe it. Madiline couldn't speak a word. She ran upstairs and started packing her clothes. " I'm going on the titanic!" she sang. Madiline could not wait for the trip tomorrow.

The air smelt musty, but Madiline did not mind. She could not wait to go on the titanic. She rushed on the ship with her mother when it was time to go. When her and her mother got on the ship, Ms. Myers gave the ticket man their tickets. He gave them their key to their room, down on the third class floor. The atmosphere seemed gloomy. Everyone was rushing to their room. Madiline and her mother finally found their room. The room was as small as her room back at home. Madiline didn't care, she thought it was great.

Time passed and it was April 14, 1912. Madiline's mother was at a third class meeting, so she wouldn't be back till later. Madiline was thinking about what they were talking about at the meeting, until a big boom interrupted her thoughts. Madiline froze as if a lion was looking at her dead in the eye. She heard people screaming outside the door. "The ship is sinking." A lady yelled. Madiline started walking as she felt freezing water touching her. She opened the door and ran out. The only thing she could think of was finding her mother. She saw a staircase and ran to it. A soft hand gripped Madiline's pale skin. Madiline instantly turned around as she saw he mothers relieved face. Before Madiline new it, she was on the top floor with her mother panting. Everyone was running to a life boat. The soft hand that was holding onto Madiline slowly slipped away. Madiline turn around with fear in her eyes. It was crowed, she couldn't see a thing. Madiline had lost her balance and fell on onto one of the life boats. The water rippled as the boat dropped onto the ice water. She was so scared she couldn't speak. The words that Madiline wanted to say wouldn't come out. As the boat started floating away, Madiline sat still. She couldn't bare that her mother is still on the ship. The titanic slowly sank, as Madiline floated away to safety.

After a while, another ship had come and put Madiline and the other survivors on the ship. The only thing she could think of was my mother's smiling face. The ship had finally made it back to my home town. Madiline couldn't believe she lost her mother. She knew this memory would scar her for life, but she knew that her mother would want her to move on with her life. Madiline followed her heart and moved on with her life.

Madiline moved into her aunt's house. Time passed and Madiline had to write an article on her point of view on the titanic. It hurt Madiline that she had to live through that memory, but she need she had to help. Madiline had put all her effort into her work. The next day Madiline noticed her story on the front of the newspaper. Madiline couldn't believe people were interested in her story. Madiline deiced she would write for her life. "Surviving a Deadly Disaster" was the best book she writes. Madiline became a famous writer. Because of her belief, Madiline had a happy life.

CHAPTER 10

1912
A Trip I Should have Skipped

By: Nakyla Brooks-Stallings

Every newsstand in town had the same first page review. Without giving it a second thought, I grabbed a fresh-printed paper with my glossy hand and ran home. The sound of my mother calling me reminded that I did something that will always get me in trouble no matter how many times I do it. "Molly, you cannot go exploring without telling me in person!" She handed me the note I left for her in the bathroom." All I can ever hear out her mouth was, "Molly, bla bla-bla bla exploring bla-bla bla-bla bla!

Before talking about what I was wearing, I pulled the warm paper from my bag. I started to read it. Once I finished, I pushed the midnight out of my pale face. She was stunned. Father came in and stared at mother. Everything happened at once. The words tied me with a rope a shot at me with larger words. I felt like I was in a western movie you see at the cinema! I picked up my dress and woke up Savannah. She was already up listening to the conversation. Her big blue eyes meet mine. "We are going on a trip!" She yelled. She bear hugged me. For an 8-year-old she squeezes hard. "We leave tomorrow for the train." I gasped for air when she let go. Speaking and not breathing is tough. "We do?!" she says. I nodded. Mother and father came to check on us. They heard her yell. "Tomorrow our équipée begins!" Mother exclaimed holding some tickets. It turned out father received them from his job.

By the break of dawn, the orange light of the warm morning sun touched my face as we walked to the train station. The smell of coal and dirt filled the air. All the posters on the torn walls were cover by mysterious eyes staring at me. Everything stood still until...BONG-BONG-DOOONG! People scurried to the train that pulled up. Mother grabbed Savanna while father went to receive the luggage. Running the crowed pushed against us like a current. Pushing back, we were the last family on the train.

The 4 day trip seemed to pass by mainly when you are drowning in a pool of thought. There were a few times I giggled through the trip because I lost my train of thought on the train. Through the murky window, the beautiful ship sat at the dock." It's magnifique!" Mother said joyfully. The train came to a halt with a jolt. The salty mist filled the air. The fish smell made me gag once we passed. Savannah was an animal person like me. She couldn't help but say, "Poor fishy!" The tall grass of people blocked the view of the ship. As if the glowing ship was calling us, we walked to see in front of us the blinding ship. A sign that said first class entrance was the entrance we went through.

From inside, the ship seemed even larger than before. The lobby was, in my mother's words, magnifique! The place was painted in gold. The stairs were as bright as the sun. The clean floors were polished to perfection. I was filling a little adventurist, so I asked," Mother, may I go explore, I promise I will be in the room for dinner." She looked at me with like she knew I would ask. "You may!" I ran to the grand deck to see if there was any one to talk to. The moment I opened to the golden doors the deck the large interior of wood was so beautiful that I cried. The smooth, polished deck reflected the crisp moon. It reminded me it was almost dinner time. I walked slowly to our room to change. I just wanted to soak up the rest of the amazement.

A strange man in a bow tie stared at me as I entered the room. "Molly, this is George. He is our servant for this trip." Father explained. "Follow me to the diner, but first, you need to dress to impress." George stared at my dress. "One moment, please!" I put on the fanciest dresses I have and ran to the door. "Let us go!" I said with sophistication. Before long we were at the dining hall. The large doors stretched to the celling. A man in an all-white outfit opened the doors. The aroma of fresh oven baked biscuits. The music filled the hall. George led us to a table. Another man came to ask what we wanted to drink. I giggled. "Is something funny?"

"No sir."

"No wine for the ladies, sir. We would like a water" Father said. I noticed he whispered to the man, but I didn't care. I bet he wanted something else to drink. He came back with 3 plates of fresh lobster legs and shrimp. "Enjoy!" His deep voice was stuck in my head as I ate. Savanna couldn't wait to eat her fish.

After a filling dinner, the happiness filled the room as people sat to listen to the wonderful music. A wail shot through the room. The captain came running to the mic and said, "THE BOAT HIT AN ICEBURG!" The trumpet blew a falling scale. There was silence in the pail room. Everyone went into a panic. Mother grabbed Savannah while I followed them to the life boats. The tricky hallways made it difficult to get there. "It has only been 4 hours since the ship let the boat. What a record!" All of the panic flowing through me has made me sarcastic. Father told me to put a sock in it. I gave him the dirty look. If I live through this, I am in BIG trouble.

Father put mother, Savanna, and me on the last life boat. Crying, I saw him take his pocket knife out. "HENRY!" Mother yelled. He cut the rope knowing he wouldn't survive. That was the last time we would see him. We couldn't believe what happened. As we watched the sea swallow, not only the boat, but our hope, love, and happiness. Not including our good clothes. A white light blinded us. A ship by the name of R.S.S. Carpathia found us. Once we were put on board, the captain supplied us with food, water, and heat. The boat sluggishly toke us home. The one thing I was afraid of was that the ship would hit the same iceberg the Titanic hit.

The R.S.S. Carpathia pulled up at the dock we left from. The familiar faces that were once happy were sad and gloomy. Everything stood still. The people made an easy path to the train station. Apparently, the news had spread. Heading home, tears burned in our eyes. All I could ask was why this happened to us. This will end family boat trips forever. The train home was unbearable. People were telling false stories about the Titanic, but that would bring back memories. I asked for some paper and a pen. I sent family members a letter say that father was went down with the ship. So long father!

Mia Kwarteng

CHAPTER II

1916
Fitting In

By: Mia Kwarteng

There it was. The Liberty Lady, as we called her back home. I was coming to America for freedom, and I could already feel its sweet, autumn, wind blowing in my face.

Screech. Boom. Our crew had just laid down the raft. At that moment, it seemed like the whole crew was creating a human tsunami. My family and I just went with the flow. Finally, it seemed like centuries before we got to check in. I thought that checking in would be the easiest part, but I was very wrong. Apparently, everybody thought that pushing and shoving was a sensible idea. When I got to what mother called the basic part of checking in, a man behind a small table asked me something in English. It sounded like "vas or nam". Mother turned to me and said, "Name."

"Shereka," I told the man. He looked at with puzzlement

in his eyes, almost as if he thought that I was stupid. He looked down and moved his pen in a way that I didn't recognize. He gave me the paper.

"Reka," he told me. That was my new name.

Out of all of us, my father was the only one who didn't pass through. He had left his birth certificate back in Russia, so he has to wait on Ellis Island until Nan sends it to him.

After passing check in and leaving Ellis Island, I forgot about one thing that all civilized people have. A home. "Mother, where are we going to stay?" I asked. She looked at me and gave me a small smirk." Uh-Oh, "I thought," trouble twenty miles ahead.

I could feel the sweat on my head from the suspense that my mom gave me. Our taxi pulled up in an upper-class neighborhood. Suddenly, we pulled up at what looked like a classically personalized house. At the door was a friendly looking man. "Daniel!" Mama shouted. I had heard many stories about Uncle Daniel.

"Welcome to my humble house" he said to me.

"You speak very good Russian," I complimented.

"Thank You," he said. I raced inside to find my own room. Luckily, I was able to find a room that was perfect.

Apparently, Uncle Daniel enrolled me into Honor Prep. Trust me, it was a shocker. As I walked into my homeroom class, I could feel all the eyes piercing through me, like ice and fire. "Hi," I tried to say in English.

"What is she trying to say?" a girl whispered. Suddenly, I

realized that she thought that I was dumb. I walked up to the girl and said something in Russian. "Uh?" she asked. I gave her my I- thought-so look, and she gave me a let's- see- who- wins this- war glare. Looks say everything.

Who knew that one person could practically ruin everything. That girl (her name is Chelsey) isn't just an ordinary kid. She's popular and evil which means that I'm in a pretty sticky situation.

At lunch, I heard my name in many conversations. I'm not sure if they were saying good or bad things about me, but I'm going to assume that they were pretty bad. I hate school.

At HP, the kids are ranked for popularity, just like people are ranked on how financially well that how are doing. I was a low average. It really sucks, doesn't it?

Ever since I left Russia, I forgot that I was Jewish. Tomorrow is Rash Hashanah, so I better get my act together before Mother notices.

It's a new day. I quickly jumped out of bed and opened my window. As, I looked down at the street, I saw a terrible sight. Chelsey Helesin had decided to stop by for a visit. It was almost as if Mama's number one rule had just slipped out of my mind. Be yourself. Just then, my brain seemed to be shaken in a jar, struck by lightning 16 times, and then dropped in a field in Switzerland after surviving a tornado. "I have to fit in," I kept on telling myself. I ran down to the kitchen and told my mom something that she had never expected to hear. "Mama, I'm not celebrating Rash Hashanah," I said.

"Are you crazy? No. Maybe you're sick!" She exclaimed. My little sister Balina looked into my eyes, almost as if she was reading my mind.

"Mama, she's serious," Balina proclaimed.

Uncle Daniel has just passed me wonderful news. Apparently, a school for foreign children has just opened up, and he enrolled me into it. As I told my sister the good news, she gave me a funny look. She said, "A school is a school. I really don't see what's so exciting about this. I just sighed and walked out of her room. Little sisters can be so dumb sometimes.

Because today is my first day at my new school, I made sure that my hair was neat, and my clothes were ironed. I expected everything to be great, and everything was. As soon as I walked through the doors, a girl came up to me. "Hi. I'm Carol. Do you need me to show you around the school?" Carol asked. I smiled. I had a fresh new start and it seemed to be going very, very well.

Rianna Gardiner
CHAPTER 12

1923
Take the correct Path

By: Rianna Gardiner

I'm stuck in here forever. Why me?! I should've listened to my mother. That's my mistake. I can't be in an overcrowded, musty, moldy, iron box for the rest of my life.

There I, Rosie Crawford was watching TV like any other thirteen year old. It was playing some boring commercial ads about jobs until I saw the most wonderful dresses on one of the models in the commercial. I just had to get it! I darted upstairs into my mom's room and asked her if I could get the dress. She gave me the worst answer a girl would ever want to hear. "No". Then at that very moment, I figured out that I don't need her permission to get the dress. Just a little letter and some money is all I need.

The letter wrote: "Hi Paul! "I was wondering if you, Bo, and Roxy would want to go to the outlet to get me one of those cool new dresses from on the TV." I know you wouldn't want to come, but I just need you to drive me there."

~ Rosie Crawford.

He definitely didn't want to go, but I didn't care! I was going to get my new dress!

One day later, Paul, Bo, and Roxy came to pick me up while my mother was at work and all of my siblings were at school. I was supposed to go too, but we were just so cool that we decided to skip school. So I got into Paul's red Model T, and we started leaving. I was so excited!

"So, how are you going to pay for this stunning new dress?" Bo acted like he never met me before, I have my ways.

"I'm getting it with money Bo." I clinched on to a small leather bag and showed Bo the money and credit card.

"Well, why does the credit card say Barbara Morano-Crawford?" Roxy was the most curious about the whole situation.

"Oh Roxy, I stole it of course, from my mother, Barbara Morano-Crawford. Paul turned around and gave me a big thumb up. He almost crashed because he paid no attention to the road. "Why thank you!" I answered.

Three hours later I arrived home. My mom was exploding red hot fury. The only reason I would think she was so mad is because I left the house without telling her. She asked me where I was all day. I had no idea if I should tell the truth or not. I guess if I lie, my mom won't be as mad. "Umm…. I was at Caroline's house." Caroline was this girl that lived down the street that my mother loved for some odd reason. I would always use her if I was in situations like this. My mother kind of cooled down a little bit, but when I walked to the stairs to go up to my room, she exploded red hot fury again, but this time it was a million times worse.

"Rosie Amanda Crawford!" "What are you wearing?!"

"It's just a dress mom."

"Yeah, a dress that is five inches too short! "Take that off young lady!" "I will not allow my child to look like a cave man!"

I think that mom got mad a little too easy. Just because in her days girls didn't wear short dresses, doesn't mean in my days we should wear long dresses. I was truly mad, so I tried getting back at her again. I grabbed the sharp torn up scissors and started cutting my hair. I thought it would be cute anyway sense everyone else wears their hair like that, but it will make mom so mad!

I thought about what happened yesterday and decided that I don't want to go through that again. But there is one problem; I can't make my hair long again! What am I going to do! I stood straight and tall with my mind blank. Then, it hit me! I remembered that for some odd reason my mom kept a bunch of wigs in her closet. I'm a genius! Just another thing I can steal from my mother.

Two days later Roxy asked me if I wanted to hang out with her and the group later. Of course I said yes. I had no idea where we were about to go and what we were going to do, but I was excited. I remembered that I had to tell my mom that I was going to Caroline's house, and then I was ready to go! I got in the car and we drove to this old place in downtown New York that had mold everywhere and rusty buildings. Roxy walked up to a metal door and knocked this special knock. I still had no clue what we were doing here. I was questioning if I should try to catch the next bus or walk home. Some big scary guy opened the door and let us in. I walked in and saw hundreds of wine bottles everywhere. I thought alcohol was illegal! Paul gave me a huge cup of brownish yellowish liquid. He told me to drink all of It in one go. I didn't want to do it, but everyone kept pressuring me. So I was about to drink it and BOOM! There were three huge officers that just broke down the huge metal door.

"Hands up where I can see them!"

Everyone put their hands up except for the two drunken people, Paul and Bessie. Right then, I heard four very loud gunshots, and two people in the room lost their lives. Were they coming for me next? After that one of the officers came towards me. I thought my life was about to end, so I squinted my eye hoping he doesn't kill me. But all he said was, "Come on youngster!" "You're coming with me!" He brought me into one of the three police cars. What am I going to do!

Once we were at the jail, the police said I could contact one family member. I wasn't sure if I was going to send my mother a letter or not. I'm pretty sure if she hears about this, she is going to flip out. I finally got the guts to letter mom. I picked up the pen, and wrote a letter to her explaining I was in jail.

Three days later I got her letter back that said. "Rosie Candice Crawford!" "What have you gotten yourself into?!" "You're lucky I love you because if I didn't, I wouldn't be bailing you out!" "Rosie, you need to follow your heart, and take the correct path."

She bailed me out the day after I got the letter, I was so excited. I didn't feel too good though. I felt horrible. I kept coughing up blood, my stomach was hurting so bad, and I had a huge cold. I thought it was something serious, so my mother rushed me to the hospital. The nurse and doctors said that if I didn't get to the hospital quick enough, I would've almost lost my life. I almost died two times, that just made me think if I was making the right decisions.

Later on, I was forced to go to rehab and therapy to make sure I don't ever drink again. It was probably worse than being in jail, or at the hospital. I spent eight months talking about why drinking was bad and ways to make sure to stop drinking. I tried telling everybody that I didn't have any drinking problems. I was under the influence, of my "friends"! But of course, no one believed me.

Once I got out of therapy, my mom took me to a Bessie Smith concert. I thought she was going to yell at me again like she always does, but I guess she was actually proud of me for being "cured". We were going on the way home, but then she made a random U-turn and turned left. When we arrived, I met with the rest of my family and we had a blast.

This one guy named Duke asked me if I wanted to do the Charleston with him. I turned and looked at my mom; she gave me a sign that meant okay. I figured out that I should take the correct path, because hanging out with those other people was a mistake. People like me for who I really am! I think my mother noticed it too, because whenever I turned and looked at her, I could see a grin on her face. I don't want to say this, but my mom was right! Ugh.

CHAPTER 13

1936
The Horrible Death

By: Alondra Villanobos-Gonzalez

Amber Meight Norman was born on May 16, 1936 in Germany. When they were on the way home from the hospital, it was below freezing and it was raining extremely hard. Amber was soaked by the time she got home. She was so purple that she looked like an oversized grape. In this current event, she got hypothermia. She was very close to losing her life. As the days got warmer, Amber grew better. During her years of growing up, she was not treated very well because she was Jewish. The way people were treating Amber hurt her, but this was all Adolf Hitler's fault. He wanted to destroy the Jewish population because they didn't have blond hair or blue eyes.

In school, her only true friend was Jenny May Waron. Jenny and Amber always stood up for each other, but during this time Jenny really had to stand up for Amber. Amber had to stop going to school because the Nazis were looking for Jewish people to kill or Jewish people to take to Concentration camps. Jenny was upset that Amber's race was being treated this way, but she went to visit amber every day to tell her that it was all going to be okay. Amber and her family had to leave their home in order to stay hidden from the Nazis.

Jenny asked her parents if Amber and her family could come and live with them until everything got fixed, and that they would come with chopper, too, their dog. Not very many people let Jews even set a foot inside their house, much less live in their house. Jenny's parents had to think about it for a while but then they finally agreed to let them live in their home. Jenny and Amber were very excited. Amber and her family were very thankful that they offered to do some work around the house but Jenny's parents decided that it would be too dangerous.

Every once in a while, Amber crept up to Jenny's room while everyone else was sleeping. While they were up there, Jenny explained to Amber about what they had learned in school and how the outdoors was like. Amber wasn't even allowed to look outside! Poor Amber looked awfully pale; she had not been in sunlight since they moved into Jenny's house. Amber felt like she was trapped in a cage but with her best friend and her family. Jenny felt so bad for Amber.

They both just decided to go outside. Who would see them anyway? They decided that night time would be better. As soon as everyone was asleep, they silently crept out. They played for a while and picked some flowers. After that, they decided that they should probably go back inside. As they turned around to go back inside they saw a man watching them. He ran over to them and grabbed Amber as soon as her saw her. "Are you Jewish!" He yelled with a voice that sounded deadly. No, I am not!" Amber replied but he seemed to notice the Star of David on her night gown. "You are a liar!" He yelled with anger in his eyes. He reached into his jacket and pulled out a gun and in less than a second he shot Amber.

As poor Jenny tried to escape, she was shot in the back and her life was gone. The Nazi soldier went in the house and he very quickly shot Jenny's parents. He looked everywhere. Then he finally found the door to the cellar. He opened it and found the two scared Jewish parents. He got them out of the house and took them to a concentration camp. They tried to escape as soon as they got there because they didn't want to suffer. They got shot, too. Both of the families died on March 3, 1943. Amber and Jenny were only 7 years old.

Ava Leaphart

CHAPTER 14

1945
The Angel of the Diamond Children

By: Ava Leaphart

"Sweetie, when you are done getting dressed, please come downstairs. We need to talk to you about something," my mom yells. I rush down in my green summer dress, white thin stockings, small heeled shoes, and my fleece sweater. It is my very favorite outfit, and today I want to look snazzy.

Everyone else in my family is already ready and at the kitchen table. They all have matching stars on their sweaters with the word Jood on it. They all are crying. Even my father and he is the strongest soldier I know. My mother walks over and pins a leather star on my fleece sweater. I smile while I ask, "another gift?" My mom is wailing now. Papa rushes over and holds her close. My brother Jood looks mad now. "Look what you have done Adina! No, these aren't gifts. These are what the German are going to use to bully us, and hurt us, and round us up to go to concentration camp for! Don't you understand? We are going to die," he yells at me.

I wanted to yell back that I am just a little girl. That I didn't know. That hated the way he acted like I should know everything, and if I don't that I'm stupid. It just wasn't fair. I needed to know now, more than ever. I needed to know why the Germans hated us so much. Did we do something to them? What is making them so violent towards us and others?

I silently grab Jood and I's book bag. He walks over to get it, but I drop it and watch him pick it up. We both walk out of the door and silently make our way to the bus. I wish I were older than 6. Maybe I would fit into my family better. We wait at the bus stop. When the bus nears our corner, I watch as the bus driver looks out the window. He slows down and I inch forward. He is my favorite bus driver, even if he is German. Then he speeds back up and drives away. Now I understand. I run to Jood and hug him while crying. I don't want to ask, but I need to know, "Jood, why did the bus drive away?" Jood looks straight ahead and says, "They hate us. He saw the star on our chests and knew we were Jewish. Now let's get to school." I silently admire how strong he is. He holds my hand all the way to school. I can tell he doesn't want to let go, but he does, and kisses me on the forehead. I know he will be there whenever I need him.

I run to my best friend Adva. All I want to hear is the sound of her soothing words. Before she can move, I grab her and grasp on tight. I cry on her shoulder. I wait to hear her words, but they do not come soothing. They came mean, and harsh, and ugly. "EW, get off of me you dirty mutt!" she screams at me. I turn around and my hair whips across her face. "Gross, you're so gross! I told you get away, so get away!" she creams at me, but this time even louder. I rush to get away from her. I can't believe she said that to me. We have been best friends since I can remember. I thought my day couldn't get any worse, but it did, and much worse.

When I got home that day I ran to my mother and cried myself to sleep while she cradled me, and whispered, "Al Fedag." Or "Don't Worry." I was whipping and turning all night as the events of my day played back in my head. I was starting to calm down when my father ran into the room, and shook me awake. "Hide my dear one!" I ran into my closet and held the door closed. My father kissed me on the forehead before locking it shut. I peer under the door, but all I can see is his bare feet, but soon even that changed. I see two pairs of black hard boots. I watch as the feet wind back and kick my father to the ground. He looks at me and cries as they beat him. Soon he is as limp as a stone. I try to keep quiet, but a small whimper escapes. The black boots head towards my closet. I try to hide in the corner, but it's no use. The men open the door and drag me out. I cry and wail as they take me downstairs. I see my mother is being held by another soldier, but I don't see Jood. The men throw us in the back of a truck. I see many other eyes in the darkness. Soon I'm lost in the small truck. With so many children calling to their moms there is no way she knows which voice is mine. I fall asleep crying and calling out. Tonight I have no dreams.

I wake up very dizzy. I can barely see anything. A girl about my age yells to the other to come over. They all pile around me. "Wait, who are you? Where is my mom?" They all look around. The small girl says, "We are in Bergen-Belson, a concentration camp. Your mother, is she Elize Chev? I guessed because she has been very worried about you. She is in another room. We would show her to you, but right now she is at work healing sick ones in another camp. She is very skilled. We will be doing the same job, but at different camps. Don't worry though, we will always be together." Soon I understand our jobs. Abby and I soon became inseparable (Abby is the girl who yelled.) Not only because we were always together. I was starting to like the concentration camp because everyone could say they knew how you felt, and they wouldn't lie. Especially when they said you would be best friends forever. Abby definitely wasn't like Adva. It was like separating us was a death wish.

When I got home that night, Abby and I became even closer. Everyone at camp gave me things to express their sorrow. I did not understand. I didn't know what had happened. Abby left for two seconds while a woman pulled her aside, and like the other women, came back sadder than ever. She cried as she explained everything, "Adina, your mother.…. She- she died! The- the soldiers took her and killed her. They lied and said that they were giving them showers! I'm so, so, so sorry." I wept on her shoulder as we lie in bed that night. Now I was officially an orphan. No one would ever want me when I got out of Bergen- Belson, if I ever did. I couldn't take anything. Not without Abby. All I wanted to do was die, just like the rest of my family.

The next week was even worse. The guards started to notice how poorly I began to work. All I could think about was my sadness. They also noticed Abby taking breaks to help me. It arose a lot of talking. About two weeks later the guards took me and Abby from our jobs. Abby refused to be stopped from helping a poor sick man she cried out his name and screamed as they carried us out. I walked poorly lowering my head barely caring. The men mumbled behind my back, "The showers or the woods?" The showers! I thought I was going to die, just like my mother, but what did the woods mean? "The woods." The other one answered, "They go with the other 54 children." 54 children I thought?! This was crazy. I tried to tell Abby, but she had started crying. The carried us to the edge of the truck, and threw us inside. There were a lot more children, a grand total of 54.

A big boy spoke out, "does anyone know what is happening?" I raised my hand and spoke, "We are headed to the woods. They will most likely shoot us dead. We are lucky they aren't gassing us." I listened the whole ride to hear what the drivers were saying. I called out near the end of the ride, "No! No! They aren't going to kill us. They are going to spare us, but they are going to leave us in the woods." They all cheered, but I didn't tell them that the men said that we were going to die of starvation in the icy woods, or frostbite. The men kicked us out of the car than drove away. We almost froze to death for a long time. I didn't keep track of the time. When it was really late at night we would cry out for help. Some of them said it was a lost cause, but it paid off.

Later a woman came. She said her name was Luba. She brought us to her home. Because there were so many of us, we all had to sleep three to a bed, and once we were all in bed, she sang us a song. I fell asleep on an empty stomach. I was really hungry for food. The next day she left early, and didn't come back until late. It was hard to tell in the darkness, but she looked like she had eaten two whole pigs! We all circled around her as we saw her empty her big coat slowly empty lots of food. We all ate a fair amount. I smiled as I slowly drifted off to sleep. The next months were just like this.

A few weeks after we got news the British soldiers were coming to liberate this camp, things got worse. Abby and I got a sickness called typhus along with a lot of the other children. The guards paid more attention to what was happening, so people stopped giving Luba things to help us survive. I would only get a bite of warm chicken about a day. We were suffering, but worst of all Abby had died. Instead of mourning again I took my sadness, and turned it into power. Will power, I fought my hardest to survive until the British came. Every week we got new updates. The soldiers became harder on us, but I refused to give up. I did it for Abby. The last week before they came was the hardest. Every day a soldier would come into the room and make sure everything was ship shape. They never caught us.

I remember the day the camp was liberated. It was liberated, April 15, 1945. I was too sick to walk, so when they saw our room a strong soldier carried me to a tent where I was safe. The doctors gave me lots of care, and soon I was healthy. I remember the soldier's strong arms carrying me, and keeping me awake. Whispering in my ear that I was free, that I was okay, but I was not. I was an orphan with no friends. The best friend I ever had was Abby, and no matter how hard I tried to forget those whole years of my life, she was always there to make me remember, either a dream at night, or during the day.

When I was healthy again, I remember Luba helping me find relatives. Almost every single one was dead. We could only find my uncle, Uncle Aaron; he treated me like his daughter. He introduced me to art. I loved it so much that I became an artist. I give half of all my earnings to Uncle Aaron. I can never forget what happened during those horrifying times in Bergen- Belson. I can't because we have reunited annually. I can never repay Luba for saving my life. I owe her everything. She was like the angel of the diamond children.

John Greene 11

CHAPTER 15

1945
The Tanjōbi (Birthday) Horrors
Hiroshima Bombing-World War II

By: John Anthony Greene III

"Mama," Hidaki yelled anxiously in a begging voice so loud
that China could hear it. "I want delicious rice rolls for
my tanjōbi" (birthday in Japanese), Hidaki declared while
he stared at the smoking hot rice rolls filling the air with
its aroma on the brown glossy table, with his plump round
eyes that were plastered on his anxious face. "Aha, it is your
tanjōbi on this fine day, and your rice rolls will be your
special treat," Mother said eloquently in a sweet, soothing voice just like a hummingbird in the mist of the fine
morning. It was just about time to go to the academy seven
blocks away. Father walked out of the bedroom, dressed for
work with his sharp polo shirt with his blue linen tie. They
walked out the house in the crisp, cold air, and trudged
through the red leaves on the sidewalk.

When they got to the academy, Hidaki heard screaming and chanting of un- melancholy kids running around the school like wild ragamuffins. "Bye, Hidaki, or should I say tanjōbi boy," Mother and Father said as they walked into the mist of the August morning to go to the Genbaku Dome 2 blocks away. Hidaki did not know that he would never see his parents alive again. Hidaki walked through the complex halls of the academy. When he got to his classroom, it was not what he expected. Broken lights dangled from the ceiling, broken blackboards stained with blood, and broken glass as sharp as needles shun on the blood-stained floor. He looked out the broken windows and saw a beautiful plane as white as snow that said in black print ENOLA GAY that soared across the crystal, clear sky. Hidaki smiled as wide as if he was getting 10 rice rolls for his birthday. Hidaki gasped for a second then BOOM! A bright light glistened through the city of Hiroshima. The light was so bright that it could burn your cornea.

Hidaki fell to the floor as his black hair flew like an airplane in the sky. A massive mushroom cloud arose above the clouds with intense heat and suffocating, dark smoke. A moderately strong force pushed Hidaki against the wood walls. Blood gradually began to drip from the back of his head because of the sharp, pointy glass. He could see out the window, all the joyful children that were playing in the yard vanished into black dust, which left a shadow in the distance. Suddenly, CRASH! The whole building from wood to metal fell on Hidaki's whole entire 9-year old body. He could even hear kids hollering and screaming in the building. Blood dripped from the old walls of the building, which was even getting inside Hidaki's mouth. Hidaki cried at the top of his lungs, "MAMA!" Black smoke filled the air as it suffocated, squeezed, and grabbed his poor throat, which filled his lungs. Suddenly the screaming and crying in the background subsided. Hidaki knew that the children's time has come to rest in the heavens and they did not have to suffer anymore which would include pain, blood and tragedy. The crystal, clear sky that cheered the morning sun was now a black darkness surrounding Hidaki.

Hidaki wondered if his parents were safe from the destruction, but when he knew that smoke completely covered the entire land, he knew that they were not going to be in the situation of being safe. Wood and blackboards were on top of Hidaki. Even a dead body plastered with blood was on top of him. The person's eyes were open, but Hidaki could see that the body was cut severely and Hidaki saw the dark intestines, the heart, and the smoke covered lungs that were from the smoke. Hidaki knew that he had to get out of this horror. Suddenly, he saw a diminutive hole that was as small as a single cell of a rat. He had to squeeze to get out of this horror, which was before his own academy where everything cheered up his day. He knew he was as plump as a pig on his grandmother's farm because he ate too much rice and beans, but this might be his life at stake if he doesn't get out of here. Hidaki pushed repeatedly, as hard as if he was in a wrestling match. Thousands of drops of sweat coursed down his worried, red face. Hidaki gradually closed his eyes as he pushed, trying not to feel the pain, and suddenly, he was lying on the ash covered ground near the academy. Debris was everywhere, which included wood, metal, and glass shattered on the destroyed piece of ground. Hidaki cried with complete joy because he could have died in what was now the building of horror, not his academy.

He caught his sight when he saw people with black and red blood coursing down their skinless backs. People were walking slowly on the horrid streets holding their eyeballs with popping veins. That is when he knew that this was not a mistake, and that plane abhorred everything in this vast land. Hidaki then went to the river to get a drink of water since he was intensely dehydrated. He saw the entire river that was completely filled with horrid blood from the dead bodies in the river and saw hopeless deceased people who were silently flowing over the dark, red blood. Hidaki in an instant moment, started feeling as melancholy as salty tears dripped down his face. Hidaki sobbed severely, until he noticed blood abruptly falling from his face. Since he was in complete shock, he slowly touched his face and felt spongy muscles and a wet slimy surface that burned so intensely that it felt like it was as hot as the sun. Black gas filled the air so it could look like a thunderstorm was occurring. Suddenly, gas went into Hidaki's nose and he started to feel like he was getting a sedative. SPLASH! Hidaki collapsed and fell into the river of horrid blood.

"Where am I," Hidaki said as he gently rubbed his worried and sleepy eyes. He could see fuzzy, coarse, and red liquid flowing in a distinctive direction as his eyes opened. Then, he saw dead bodies curled up like his green, cute turtle, Kazmamo when he reposes. Hidaki screamed so loud that Africa could hear it. Hidaki Tono suddenly turned over and suddenly saw his parents floating in the river with their big brown eyes wide open. Hidaki smiled as if the bombing never even happened. He can imagine his mother and father waking up and his life would go back to the way it was, but that probably wasn't true. His mother had her beautiful blue linen skirt and her beautiful red blouse, but it was stained with blood. Mama, Papa," Hidaki said softly and gently while he shook them repeatedly, and the particular action made them have a San Francisco Earthquake inside, but stood still like a statue with their eyes wide open.

Hidaki's poor heart started to palpitate so fast that it was getting ready to burst and to shed blood on the destroyed shore of the river. Hidaki then sobbed so hard that he was getting ready to past out again. "MAMA, PAPA! My tanjōbi, my rice rolls," Hidaki, sobbed. Hidaki hugged their deceased bodies trying to fight back the tears, but the tears won the fight. Hidaki Tono was now parentless and had to mourn and to be in the world of depression in solitude.

Hidaki's parents were silently working at the mighty Genbaku Dome. "Takeo, I need to get those papers in less than 3 hours so I can go home for my son's tanjōbi," Mother said. The mother suddenly smiled that warmed the workers' heart then BOOM! The joyful spark of the Genbaku Dome was gone and the horror crept in. The entire building rattled so abruptly and dangerously, like an earthquake was going on. Just because of the environment around Hidaki's mother, she knew that her poor son was not going to be okay. A single tear rolled down her face. In an instant, both of the parents saw people covered with blood and severely broken necks. Single heads were lying on the ground because they were decapitated by the strong force of the mushroom cloud. Suddenly, strong gravity pulled the parents out of the building through the windows. Everything from glass to debris was stuck on their throats. They were half-dead in the crisp, cold air on that August morning. The mushroom cloud rose in the air with bright light and smoke covering the sky. Then, SPLASH! They landed in the river, hitting hard stone where they bled to death.

"I lost everything!" Hidaki yelled at the top of his little lungs. He came out of the river drenched with aqua (water), crying like a newborn baby that just entering the world. He remembered his mother and father tucking him in at nightfall in his own warm bed with the fluffy and comfortable blanket that his grandmother crocheted. He sobbed even more, where the tears coursed down to create a big puddle in the middle of the bloodstained streets. He looked up and saw that plane soaring through the air. The noise sounded like someone had leaves in their throat while they spoke. "That is the plane that messed up my whole life," Hidaki thought. "I abhor you," Hidaki yelled. He went down to his knees and cried. Those pilots didn't care in the world if his parents died on his side in that river and in front of his poor eyes. Hidaki pondered if all of this disaster was his birthday present from that plane. His mother had told him that a war was going on, and a country called the U.S. abhorred the country of Japan. Was the plane the enemy after all? As Hidaki went down to his knees in the bloody streets of Hiroshima while water dripped down his shirt, people were sadly lying on the streets. Hiroshima, Japan would now have to be depressed in solitude on this day of August 6, 1945.

Buildings were terribly destroyed; houses were in blazing orange flames that lit up Hidaki's pupils and fires dispersed across the land. Suddenly, he saw his home. He saw his green little turtle with a broken shell and a broken neck. Hidaki's warm blankets and toys burst into flames, never to be seen again. Soon, he saw the Genbaku Dome in big flames, right next to the river of blood. There was a small broken building with a red cross plastered on its side. It was a HOSIPTAL!! Hidaki cheered with joy. No matter if he was so far away, he could still hear the moaning of the injured. Hidaki then ran as fast as a cheetah in the savanna in Africa until suddenly, BOOM! Hidaki collapsed less than 1 foot away from the hospital. Suddenly, two injured men picked Hidaki up with their burned arms and hands struggling to bear.

When Hidaki started rubbing his eyes roughly, he saw people with blood plastered on their faces and their bodies. Even the people working were injured severely "Tanjōbi, Hidaki yelled at the top of his brittle lungs so loud that the U.S can hear it. Suddenly, people were looking at him distinctly strange. Hidaki then sobbed so much that his whole sheet was damp. Hidaki Tono was one of the only children that survived the bombing.

Hidaki Tono grew older and lonely as the days went by and Hidaki had to be depressed in solitude as he felt like he was being severely punched repeatedly thousands of times through his life. He did not get to see his bride at his wedding because he was so heartbroken. He did not get to see his parents smile at his children. Hidaki could not even have children because the radiation infected his reproductive system from so long ago. Surrounding him, silence filled his home in Tokyo, Japan. No children saying "DADDY," was around him. He lost everything at a very young age, which was known to be 9 years old. Even at 76 years old, he could still remember his parents floating in that river, dead with their eyes open.

Hidaki Guiro Tono decided to go to Hiroshima to see the improvement. There in Hiroshima, it was nothing like his old home and it was definitely not like 1945. Bright lights dispersed across the city where cars went on the roads as fast as if they were on a racing track trying to win first place. Skyscrapers stood up tall and strong in the distance, so high that it reached the clouds. And there near the river of his mother and father's grave, stood proudly was the Genbaku Dome where Hidaki's parents had worked since the day Hidaki turned 4 years old. It was now a Bomb Dome. When Hidaki saw that sight, the thought came back to his mind of his parents lying dead on that same river and the same location, and he shed a tear that coursed down his face. That horrific day on his own birthday would always haunt his mind for the rest of his life. Hidaki knew that no matter if he did not have any family or friends to support him through his challenges in his life, though they would forever be in his broken heart. He still wonders if that was his present from the enemy, which was the United States of America that didn't care in the world if all those innocent Japanese, which included his parents, had to suffer, and died. Thankfully, Hidaki did survive and will live on with the fears of August 6, 1945.

Notes

• Tanjōbi - means birthday in the Modern Japanese

adriana Otero

CHAPTER 16

1954
Nicolle's Big Rebellion

By: Adriana Otero

"Mama" 11 year old Nicolle said." I want to try."

"Try what honey?", asked her mother.

"I want to try to be like those people ", said Nicolle. "But how are they so brave? All I want to do is maybe try a sport or make a difference", declared Nicolle. Nicolle wanted to make a change of some sort. She just had to find that thing in her life. Finally she got it! She wanted to make a group or an organization to stand up to people or unfair laws like Rosa Parks did on the bus. Nicolle realized the major thing in her life and for others was her education. When Nicolle looks outside, she sees a huge building with stainless glass windows and bricks as red as fire. That is an all white's school. But when she looks at her school, she sees an old cabin painted white with a leaky roof and no widows.

The next day as Nicolle was looking through the newspaper she said "Another one of those groups has been started mama. The paper says it is called the civil rights movement ", said Nicolle. That's when she realized she had to start the group. She just had to get everyone at school to agree. That was going to be hard because many of them did not even know that they were getting poorly educated. Nicolle thought she had a poor education. Her school had leaks and it was really crowded. A building meant to hold 130 people was holding 450 people. Also she knew that learning basic multiplication facts in 5th grade was not average. When she heard about the Little Rock 9 she realized that she might actually have a chance to open up that all white school.

The only problem for Nicolle was getting the parents to join in on this. She had already talked to her mother about this idea. Nicolle also sent some flyers home with a few people to tell their parents. Before she knew it Nicolle had about 70 parents signed up. That number wasn't enough for her though. She felt like giving up on this. When she heard Martin Luther King Jr.'s speech she realized that she couldn't give up now. The next day Nicolle made about 450 flyers to go home with students. Finally she had almost the entire school signed up. This plan was far from over. She had to think of a date that everyone would be free. "Maybe I will do it next Saturday. Nah! It would be such a late notice because today is already Thursday. Maybe the Saturday after next Saturday. That's perfect! Now I just have to spread the word." Nicolle thought as she pondered the idea.

The next day at school Nicolle happily skipped into the teachers' classroom to tell them to remind their students about the meeting. During class Nicolle was playing with her silky white dress her mama made her. She sat right next to the teacher. Nicolle was just waiting for the teacher to say the important announcement. It seemed like forever. She watched the clock tick. Hours passed. Finally at the end of the day the teacher said that the group would be meeting next Saturday. Nicolle was so happy. She couldn't believe that what she was doing was a success. As the next week went by, Nicolle and her mom thought of some more things to include in the meeting. Finally it was Saturday. Nicolle wouldn't stop jumping with excitement and a little fear. When she thought almost everyone was there they started the meeting.

"Come on guys. This secret meeting has to stay a secret", Nicolle whispered softly. "If other people find out, they might tell the police and we might get busted! Anyways, here is the plan. Next Wednesday after math, the parents will meet us right outside of the school. We will not leave there until they give us equality!" Nicolle said rightfully. When everyone went home, Nicolle just sat there and hoped for the best. For she was nervous and fearful, she still knew she could do it.

As Wednesday came, Nicolle got prepared for what was going to happen. When she got outside, she was flabbergasted to see so many people already out there. When Nicolle walked into that school, she automatically felt like a new person. "Hey Mister" Nicolle said as she and the group walked into the front office.

"I want to speak to the principal now!" Nicolle's mom said. Lots of people started yelling at them to get out.

"We don't want to use violence but we will if we have to", one of the other parents said. When the principal came, they told him that they wanted him to open the school up to African Americans.

"In my dreams", said the principal.

"Well I guess we won't move until you give us equality," said one of the parents.

Two days passed and nothing happened. They were just feeding on the ninety-six sandwiches one of the parents brought. It was a really tough time. Finally it was Friday. The principal was tiered of them. Barely anyone went to school that day because of them. They were all complaining but they weren't going to give up.

"Fine. I'll call the Board of Education… right after I call the POLICE!" said the principal. Everyone gasped. They automatically heard sirens getting closer and closer. It was a spine tingling feeling for Nicolle when the men in blue walked in.

"It's all a misunderstanding officer. We just want the right to send our children to school here," said Nicolle's mother. They refused to be arrested. The cops tried to get them all in hand cuffs, but they did not have enough. They started dragging people out of the building. They were yelling at them at the same time. Their cruel, vicious words crept into Nicolle's little ears and made her heart feel like it never had before. It was that feeling that you get when you know something really bad is happening. By the sixth person they dragged out, they were already tired of it. The officers' cold hard fingers wrapping around them and picking them up. That was the worst feeling ever. It was like a harsh blast of an arctic storm picking you up and dragging you down a steep mountain. As they tried to drag more people out, everyone started shouting, as if they were about to die, because of the officers. The officers couldn't handle such a big group of people, but they weren't leaving without a fight. They called in more officers to help them get all of those people out of there. All the officers did was try to at least pull some people out of the way. They only managed to get 20 people out before they surrendered.

"Wow. Not even the cops could get you out of here. I guess I really do have to call the Board of Education don't I?" said the principal. They listened gathered around the principal as he called the Board of Education, just to make sure. The Board of Education fought long and hard to try not to integrate the school. One harsh sentence after the other. Finally the Board of Education's plans backfired. A few days later they filed it. Finally Nicolle and her friends could live in peace and go to school happily with people of different races. Although it took a while for them to adjust and make new friends, it worked out perfectly at the end. It was Nicolle's goal to be with other races. Now her dream has come true.

CHAPTER 17

1964-1968

Silenced!!

By: Mariam Drammeh

"No, this is impossible! Why would they say something like that? This time it has gone too far." I cannot believe those racist scientists dared to make accusations like that. How could their studies show that whites are smarter than blacks?? I'm just as smart as any white kid! I threw that newspaper to the ground and stomped on it with all my might. I could not bear to look at it anymore.

Suddenly, the door burst open. Mama brutally slammed it back to a close. Mama is such a calm person; she's never done anything like that before. "Mama, what's wrong?" I asked worriedly. "Segregation is what's wrong! I should've known!" Mama cried out. She has never been this angry before. Look what segregation has gone and done to her! "Mama, please calm down! What happened to you?" I tried to settle her down as I spoke. "I walked right into that job interview and the boss said, "I suppose you go home, because I've never hired a black." Tears started to course down her cheeks. I started to cry to, but these were tears of pure, burning red rage. "C'mon baby, let's go to the park. That will burn off some steam." Mama soothed me as she usually does so well. "I guess we both need some air." I answered quietly.

The park's scenery was breathtaking. "Charity, Charity!" Sarah called. Sarah sprinted over to where Mama and I were standing. "Did you not hear me?" Sarah asked. "I'm pretty sure the whole park heard you!" I joked. Sarah was my best friend in the whole world. Nothing could separate us, not even segregation. "Charity, has something got you down?" Sarah asked. She was concerned about me. "This whole system of segregation got me down! It just ain't fair! You don't understand you're white." Words spilled out of my mouth like a fountain. I wasn't even thinking about how I might've hurt poor Sarah's feelings. "I...I'm sorry. I didn't mean to say it like that." I apologized. I truly was sorry, I had spoken harshly. "It's okay Charity. You must be going through a lot." Sarah understood me. I sure was lucky to have a friend like her.

"Sarah Marie Mitchell! What do you think you are doing?" Ms. Mitchell was screaming. Her face was as red as a blazing fire. "Mom, this is Char" Sarah was stopped mid-sentence. "I don't care who she is! She's black! I never want to see you with this dirty black child again! Come on, let's go!" Ms. Mitchell shouted. I was completely and utterly shocked and I was about to blow like a volcano. "Well maybe, you're a racist, disgusting human being! You're the humiliation, not me! Are you just going to stand there and judge me by my color, not my character? What kind of monster are you?" I screamed. I was furious. I could not take the racism. Ms. Mitchell was shocked by my choice of words and with that, she stormed off with Sarah. As they walked away, I could see through Sarah's eyes that she was truly sorry.

I sobbed my eyes out and dropped myself onto the nearest bench. I could not believe what Ms. Mitchell had said to me. I lost my best friend in the whole entire world, because of that lady, that racist woman. What was I to do? "Charity, Get up!" Mama commanded. I turned around and looked at the sign on the bench. In big black letters it read, "Whites Only." I was fed up. I would not succumb to this. "No, I will not get up." I announced. Mama did not tolerate this. She yanked me off the bench and pulled me home. "Charity, you must get used to segregation, because it ain't ending any time soon!" Mama told me and I sure knew it.

Summer soon fell into fall, Mama found a job as a waitress at the all black café. I found some new friends who were also strong about segregation. Life seemed to be turning to the better side. Hopefully, it would last.

The autumn breeze whipped across my face. I was completely overjoyed. I love school and I hope segregation doesn't ever get in the way of that. We walked into Chestnut Middle School and it was mighty big. Right there in front of Mama and I was the principal. His smile was warm and made me feel happy. "Are you our new janitor?" He asked Mama. What? "Well, no sir. I am here to enroll my daughter." Mama answered the principal with a straight face, but I could tell that she knew this wasn't going to end well. "I'm sorry mam, but we don't accept black children." The principal spoke to us in a clear voice and I was starting to see the horrible side of him, the racist side. I tried to speak, but I couldn't. This time I understood what was happening. Segregation had taken over this country. It was time for me to do something about this. And I was going to make sure folks knew it.

"Okay y'all, here's the plan. At 3:00 pm we all march in front of Chestnut Middle School. Holding signs, screaming, whatever it takes to get noticed. We have to get this system abolished. Forever. Who's with me?" I explained my plan to my friends. It was crazy, but crazy enough to work. "Me!" My friends shouted with excitement. For the rest of the time, we made protest signs. Soon enough, we were ready. "Let's do this." I announced.

Gathering around the front of the building, we started our protest. "We will not be limited! We have power!" All of us chanted. A crowd started to gather. It was time for my speech. "Blacks shall not be limited by the color of our skin. What is wrong with you, to judge us by a characteristic we were born with? How dare you?! Just because you racially discriminate against us, rob us of our personal freedoms, does not mean we will give up! Blacks will not be silenced!" I screamed my powerful words so everyone could hear it. By the time I finished speaking, I noticed that someone had called the police. That meant trouble.

The police looked at us with horrid eyes. They were prepared to unleash whatever they had on us. Some of my fellow protesters looked at me with fear in their hearts. We had been too far to leave now. The police men started hitting us with rocks and sticks. Blood and tears flowed slowly down our body, but neither our pain, nor our fear would stop us. "We will not be silenced! We will not be silenced!" We chanted. I didn't care that fierce pain was in our arms and legs. I will never be silenced. Soon, I heard the sharp, short barks of vicious police dogs. Next

thing I knew they were chasing after us and there needle
like teeth were piercing into our skin.   My body ached
with terrible pain, and I was getting dizzy from the loss of
blood, but that will never stop me.   BAM! The school door
was slammed open.   "Stop! For now on Chestnut Middle
School is desegregated!" The principal yelled.   I cheered.
Finally my message is starting to be heard.

July 7, 1965

Radio music blasts through my home, we are all joyful
today.   Just a year ago, segregation was outlawed.   America
had come to its senses.   They finally knew that you cannot
silence blacks, and you can definitely not silence me, Charity Morton.

CHAPTER 18

1965
Will We Ever Be Equal?

By: Jasmine Santos

"Mom, will we ever be equal?" I asked. Daisa thought that all of this commotion was really unnecessary. She didn't understand why all of this was happening.

"Honestly sweetie, I don't know. All I know is that I'm going to try to make this family happy again."

"Okay Mama", Daisa said with a really gloomy face. Daisa couldn't stop thinking if she would ever make white friends. I mean would she? She knew that she couldn't do anything at all with the whites. She was so confused. She felt like she was lonely. Like she has no one she can depend on. Daisa knows that she has her mom, but she thinks that she can't even depend on HER! Daisa knew there had to be something good come out of all of this commotion. Although she was scared to know what that good thing was, she was always open minded.

"Goodnight Mama", Daisa uttered.   Then, she hopped in bed.

"Isn't it a beautiful day outside?" Mom questioned as she hiked through the park.

"It sure.. uh oh!" She could NOT believe what she saw. Golden blonde hair, white skin, and crystal blue eyes.   It was GWEN! Daisa saw that Gwen looked at her.

"What's wrong Daisa?" Mom wondered.

"It's Gwen.   She's been bullying me since the day she first saw me.   And she only bullies me because of my skin color, Mom.   It gets really annoying, and it is really bothering me.   She wouldn't want me to do that to her, would she? Am I even WORTH IT?" Daisa said while shedding tears.

"Honey, don't say that!! That girl is just being unfair and rude! You are totally worth it! There are many people in this world who love and care about you! You have me, and you have your siblings.   Don't ever say that again!"

Daisa walked home.   But... there she was again.

"Hey! I don't think you should be out in the sun.   You're already dark enough! Hahaha!!"

I couldn't help but cry! Did she even realize what she was doing to me? Did Gwen even care? That's what I wonder all the time.   It worries me a bunch.   I want to have a good reputation.   I don't want people to abhor me.   I think that I was born for a reason.   Everyone was.

When Daisa got home, she went straight to bed.   She felt very unhappy.   She really didn't like to feel like she was unimportant. She always wanted people to like her she knew that there would be people who didn't like her, but she tried hard for that not to happen.

Once again, Daisa went to the park, just like any other day. It felt toasty outside. Daisa always enjoyed that weather. But then, she suddenly felt like it was ice cold outside.

"NOT AGAIN!!" Daisa said with her heart beating 100,000,000 beats per minute. "It's her. Why is this happening?" Daisa heard Gwen giggling from 5 miles away. She came closer, closer, and even closer. Until she could finally see her crystal clear. Gwen looked at Daisa in disgust. Like always, there was poor, ruthless Daisa, crying on her knees. At that point, Daisa thought that her mom was a liar. She thought that Gwen was right, Daisa was NOT good enough. She was not worth it.

When Daisa got home, of course her mom noticed that Daisa was crying.

"Are you crying because of that Gwen girl?" There was silence.

"What did I tell you about her? She is just being a rude and cruel little girl. You know you are worth it, and your family loves you!"

"It's too late Mama. I know you're just trying to make me happy. If I was a stranger to you, you would probably think the same thing. I've already been stabbed in the heart too many times!" Mom walked away feeling heartbroken. But then, she turned back around and said:

"By the way, your cousin has been sorted into the white race. He's going to treat our family like Gwen's treating you now. You better get used to it." Daisa's heart dropped.

Why would her cousin do that to her? She really thought that he loved her.

A few days passed and Daisa was trying to keep in touch with her cousin. Although, she doesn't even know why she tries. He just keeps on ignoring her. It's not like he wants to. He just doesn't have a choice.

"Daisa... you sad yet?" Daisa immediately knew who it was. It was Gwen. Daisa thought that Gwen had heard about her cousin being sorted into the white race. She really didn't want Gwen to know about that...

"Come on! Answer me Daisa!"

"Okay Gwen, I will answer you. I am sad... because of you! You've treated me so differently because of my skin color. Is that really appropriate? We were all created to be equal. You wouldn't want me to treat you like you treat me. Would you? I'm tired of everything you do to me. And what's not fair is that I treat you like I would treat anyone of my race! You don't even realize what you do to me." Daisa knew that she had a point. Everyone was created to be equal. Not one race with more power than the other.

There was a long pause. I mean like a REALLY long pause.

"You know what, you're right Daisa. I shouldn't treat you differently because of your skin color. We were created to be equal. I really wouldn't want you to treat me like I treat you, and I didn't realize what I was doing to you. I'm sorry for treating you like you're not good enough."

"It's okay, but can we just start over and be friends?"

"Of course! I would really like that." And they walked away laughing.

CHAPTER 19

1968
Mama, Pa, Henry and I

By: Lundon Shields

"Hey farmer girl!" they tease. "Why don't you come by my house later and plant some strawberries!" She taunts. The other girls giggle. It doesn't work like that. I think. It takes time and strawberries don't even grown this season. I want to yell. But I don't. I know that if I do, they'll just laugh and call me even more hurtful names. So I just stay quiet.

"Hey Jess! How was school today?" Henry greets from the field.

"Fine" I shrug. I don't want to tell him or Mama and Pa about what really goes on at school. They already have more than enough problems. Sometimes I wonder how come everyone else has so much more money than my family. It's almost like the Great War just magically made some people rich. It doesn't make sense. It doesn't seem fair.

The next day goes by like any other. But this time, the teasing is worse. Why was I thought of as so different? Just because I work and live on a farm? Is it because their families have more money than mine? Do Mabel and Ruth get teased like this? But then I stop myself. I already know the answer. And I know why.

The weeds make weird noises as I uproot them and toss them into a small bin. This, of all the chores we do on the farm, this is my least favorite. As I'm working on the last few weeds, I see two feet walking toward me. I'd recognize those shoes anywhere!

"Mabel!" I leap up. I haven't seen her in what seems like forever! We've been best friends longer than anyone can remember. But we don't get to play much because we both have tons of chores on the farm. She doesn't go to school with me either because she's home schooled.

"Mama, why can't I have school at home like Mabel and her brothers?" I ask one night at dinner. Tonight, we have my favorite meal of Mama's: Chicken, green beans and mashed potatoes.

"Well, honey at a school like the one you go to, you'll get a better education than with me and Pa." she explains. "We want the best for you and Henry so you can get a better education and lead a better life than what I and Pa have."

"And hopefully not have to work on some farm either." Pa chimes in. Mama gives him a funny look. The one where she wants to be mad, but can't help but laugh. It always makes me and Henry giggle.

"And maybe Mabel's parents are really smart or have some teaching experience." He adds.

"But why do you ask? Is there something wrong at school?" Mama asks a concerned look on her face. I think for a moment. Should I tell her? Should I tell her about all of the endless name calling? "Yes." I mumble. "There is something wrong."

"Well what is it honey? Is it too hard?" I wait for a moment. "Well there are these girls at school that call me mean names like 'farmer girl' and 'colored'." I mutter. I didn't want to tell her but I had to! I just couldn't take it anymore! Everyone is quiet for a few long moments.

"Oh. I'm sorry sweetie! Why didn't you tell us? How long has this been going on?" Mama says breaking the silence. "Almost two months."

"What?!" Mama cries. I frown. I really don't like to make her upset.

"I don't know." I shrug. I guess I was just scared.

The next day, Mama keeps me from school. I stay at home and work on the farm. We're planting asparagus this season! My favorite!

"Hey Jess, how you comin' along on those crops?" Henry shouts from across the field.

"Almost done!" I yell. Henry's stopped going to school too. Mama and Pa are worried that he's bein' bullied too. So they took him out.

"Hey guys, you'll have to hurry up with those crops and come on in in a few!" Pa calls from the porch, "heard there's gonna be a dust storm later on."

"Okay! Just let us finish these last few!" Henry shouts back. But only a few short minutes later, I hear a low rumbling. Shortly after, I see it. A huge, thick brown cloud about a mile away quickly getting closer and gaining speed.

"HENRY! I yelp across the field. But he's nowhere to be found. After a couple of minutes, he's still missing and the cloud is drawing closer and closer. What should I do? Go warn Mama and Pa of the early storm? Look for Henry? Wait? Maybe I should go inside. What if he's there? But then I look up and see the monster cloud creeping in closer and closer to the farm. And in front of it, I see him; he's covered in dust and dirt, trudging along towards the farm.

"Henry! Come on!" I wave him over frantically. Soon, he reaches the farm and we rush inside to a worried Mama and Pa. When we come inside, no questions are asked but I know there will be later.

"C'mon, c'mon! Hurry!" Pa says in a frantic voice as he leads us out back to the underground safety shelter. One by one we file into safety. As soon as everyone is accounted for and safe, the questions pour over us like the rain we never get.

"Where were you? What were you doing? Are you okay?" I can answer these easily but I don't know about Henry. Besides, he's in the corner coughing like a mad man!

"Henry!" Mama cries. "What's wrong?" But he can't speak.

Luckily, Henry stops coughing long enough for us to get him to a doctor when the storms over. I hope he's okay.

Fortunately, the doctor says it's only a bit of dust in his lungs and can be cleaned by drinking water and staying inside. "But where are we supposed to get water from?" Mama asks. She's right. It barely rains here.

"Oh! That's right." The doctor exclaims. He reaches behind his wooden desk and pulls out a couple containers of water. Pa hesitantly reaches out for them.

"So…how long will it take him to recover?" Pa questions as he shifts uncomfortably with the containers. The doctor thinks for a moment. "Hmm about two to three weeks." He nods. I look around at everyone. They all look worried.

Later in the day after Henry is settled, we start to clean up. It seems like an eternity of boring labor but its needed and soon it's finished.

Henry seems to be getting better but not fast enough. I hear Mama and Pa whispering about some men that take peoples farms, but I don't see why they would take ours. Wouldn't they give us another chance? Would they even care that we don't have enough people working on the farm at the moment? I really hope so.

After another whole week, Henry still hasn't been able to help on the farm. It's been two weeks. Mama and Pa whisper about the man more and more.

A whole 'nother week passes as summer slowly fades into fall. Henry has been doing better but Pa says he won't be able to help until mid-October. Every week I hear more and more of those men, I fear them. This afternoon I saw mama go to the mail office. I wonder who she's writing too.

For days in and days out, very little is done on the farm. Occasionally, we can sell a few crops but not enough. I hope the men don't notice.

KNOCK, KNOCK, KNOCK! I bolt up in my bed. "I think it was just a dream" I think. Then, they happen again just as I'm about to nod off to sleep. A few seconds later, I hear Pa shuffle to the door. When it creaks open, I hear an unfamiliar voice. But then I realize it's not so unfamiliar. Uncle Joe! I desperately want to go see him because I haven't since I was a baby but I wait until Pa tells me I can. When he opens my door, I hear something completely unexpected: "Jess, Hurry up and pack your things. Were leavin'."

"To go to Uncle Joe's?" I ask hopefully.

"Just pack." He tells me. And with that, he shuts the door. I'm confused but I pack my few belongings anyway. But what about Mabel? And Ruth! I think as I gather my clothes. Where are we even going? I wonder as I pack my dolls into a bag. Once I finish packing, I join Mama, Henry and Pa. "Ready?" Mama asks with a weak smile.

"Yes." I say. But I'm not even sure if I really am. We walk to a train station about two miles away that I never even knew we had. When we board, it's nearly morning and the sun peaks over the horizon. Everyone seems tired.

It seems like we've been riding forever but Pa says it's only been two hours. After about another hour, the train slows to a stop.

"Here we are!" Uncle Joe says brightly. "Sort of." Turns out that we have to walk two more miles to our destination.

Once we arrive, I see a well-built house sitting on top of a

106

bright green hill that's almost two times the size of ours.

"Well" Pa says as he pats Henry and me on the back. "This is our new home."

"Well w-what about the farm?" I stutter. Pa just stands there for a while.

"That's our past. The farm is long gone." He finally says. He grabs our hands and we walk toward our new house, our new home and our new life. Just Mama, Pa, Henry and I.

Cooper Clickner

CHAPTER 20

1975
Vietnam Evacuation

By: Cooper Clickner

All the talk recently is about the Vietnam War. It was dangerous and costly for the brave soldiers who fought. No one really thinks about the Vietnamese. People only think about how it affected Americans. People never really think about how awful it was for the Vietnamese. They suffered huge losses, and Aiden and his family were among these people.

Aiden is 11 years old. He lives in Saigon, the capitol of South Vietnam. He goes to Antiminh Middle School. For his whole life, he has been exposed to the dangers of the Viet Cong. All he knows is to stay inside the city and to never go wandering off. He doesn't want to either. He has heard the stories of other village raids by the Viet Cong. They steal all of the village's stuff and then they burn it down. If they find anyone alive, they kill them.

Aiden has never actually encountered them though, until now.

One day, Aiden's town was attacked by the Viet Cong. Luckily, Aiden's family wasn't hurt. In the middle of the attack, a U.S. soldier came to rescue Aiden and his family from the heart of the attack. He safely escorted them to the safety of their home. When he was safe at home, Aiden asked "What's your name?" to the U.S. soldier.

"Skid," the soldier replied. "I work for the U.S. army to protect you. I am here to help you stay alive. What's your name?"

"I'm Aiden," Aiden said.

"Cool. Well I'm glad you didn't get hurt. I have to go save other people now," Skid said.

"Bye!" Aiden exclaimed. Skid then rushed to go save another family in peril.

"We have to get out of here," said David, Aiden's dad to the family of three.

"I agree," said Judy, Aiden's mom.

"The U.S. is losing the war," David exclaimed. "They are going to evacuate soon. We need to catch a flight out."

"I see," Judy stated. "You are afraid of a raid on Saigon after the soldiers leave."

"Yes," David replied. "I plan to leave when they leave. That may be next year, or it may be just a few days away."

The next day, while Aiden was at Antiminh Middle School, his parents came to get him. "We're leaving Vietnam,"

Judy told Aiden. "We'll catch one of the early flights. We need to leave right now!"

"I hope we can catch a flight," thought Aiden. He didn't know it at the time, but this evacuation could save his life. If he didn't catch a flight, his family would be left behind. They will then be vulnerable to Viet Cong raids more than ever.

When Aiden's family lined up to evacuate, they met Skid. "Hello Aiden," Skid said. "We're evacuating today. Would you like to come with me?"

"Sure!" Aiden happily exclaimed. "Can my parents come too?"

"Absolutely!" Skid said. "Come on, follow me." Aiden sprinted to follow Skid, with his family in hot pursuit. While he ran, Aiden noticed Skid had a lot of medals.

"Wow, you have so many medals Skid. You must be a superstar!"

"Why thank you, but I'm just an average person, just like you!" Right as Skid finished, the four of them arrived at the helicopter.

"Quick, get in before it takes off!" Skid said. THUMP! THUMP! The helicopter shook whenever someone got in. It was like entering a river raft.

After everyone who had lined up to evacuate had gotten into a helicopter, Skid jumped in the one with Aiden and his family. Skid then said into a walky-talky "Everyone's in. You're clear for take-off." The helicopters then took off for the U.S.

The next day, Saigon was captured by the North Vietnam Army and the Viet Cong. They burned buildings and killed civilians. Aiden and his family safely evacuated, but his friends did not.

You see, no one thinks about the Vietnamese. Most people think about how the Vietnam War affected us. Sure, it changed us, but it also effected people like Aiden and his family. Aiden didn't suffer that much, but he did have to leave behind his friends and family. That is just sad enough, but not all of his friends may have survived the raid.

CHAPTER 21

2001
And the Towers came Crashing Down

By: Lillian Rodgers

My name is Emma Rose. I had an interview at the South Tower at the World Trade Center on September 11, 2001. It was very traumatic, but I survived and that's all that matters.

It all started on a nice, sunny day on September 11. I woke up, got ready, and headed towards town. It was the day I was getting an interview at the biggest towers in Manhattan, New York. I stepped outside in a pencil skirt and a fancy tank top. I wore velvet maroon high heels that matched my earrings and necklace. I stepped to the curb and put my hand out. A mustard yellow cab rolled up slowly.

I opened the door to the cab and put one foot in at a time. The taxi driver called back to me and gave me a questioning look through the rear view mirror. I excitedly asked him, "Please take me to the South Tower in the World Trade Center." He then replied, "That will be ten bucks." I pulled out the cash and laid it in his right hand. He pulled away from the curb slowly, but accelerated when we got back on the street.

After dropping me off, the cab driver gave me a smile and zoomed off like a bee. I stepped up to the doors of the South Tower when my phone rang. I looked at it to see it was my best friend Sam. I held the silver cased iPhone to the side of my head hoping this was important. A high pitched voice echoed in my ears. I could hear Sam talking with a mixture of nervousness and excitement. She spoke about how she had an interview at the North Tower that morning. I confidently told her congratulations and that I was busy. I waited for a second, and then heard the buzzing tone after.

I slowly pulled my phone away from my head, reached out my hands, and allowed myself in. I walked up to the front desk and told the receptionist I had an interview. She directed me where to go and I listened. I nervously stepped into the elevator with three other people; all tall and formal looking. I pressed the button the size of my thumb on the side of the door that read, 100. I waited patiently with butterflies in my stomach until the old, rusty lift stopped at my destination. I stepped out repeating the door number in my head over and over.

I finally came upon a wood door that had the number twelve engraved in it. I twisted the handle to the left and it welcomed me in. I took a seat in front of a rectangular wood desk. I stared at the navy blue wall and a woman in black flats walked in. She startled me at first, but I felt relaxed seconds later. The woman was tall with pride and walked with confidence. She stepped in and closed the wooden door. She took a seat in the green chair behind the desk and told me, "Hi." "My name is Linda Vandoch." "I will be your interviewer today."

We stared into each other's hazel eyes for a long moment. We finally broke contact when she said, "First question, why would you like to work at the South Tower?" Before I could reply, I looked out the window and saw a Boeing 767-200 flying across the sea blue sky right at Linda and me. I wanted scream, but before I could, one of the wings collided with the window. Glass flew everywhere. Everything in the small room fell, including me. I eventually woke up and realized I had been unconscious. I rolled over and saw a huge piece of glass the size of a composition notebook sticking out of Linda's head. Blood red as wine dripped from the huge cut upon her face. I rolled back over shutting my eyes so I wouldn't be frightened. With the courage of my heart and the strength of my bones, I got up and stumbled towards the wooden door.

When I finally reached the silver doorknob, I twisted it to the left and it swung open. I got maybe three feet in the hallway when I saw the same person I saw in the elevator earlier. She reached out her weak, dirtied hand towards me and I did the same. Suddenly, her hand limped. I looked up to see the life taken out of her face and I looked back down as crystal clear tears trailed down my cheeks. I sat up and glared at the elevator. I hoped that Sam was okay. I went back in my thoughts and remembered the phone call this morning. I refocused and dragged my body towards the elevator. When I finally reached the elevator, I collapsed. Managing to reach the numbers, I pushed 1 and the elevator doors closed.

When the rusty lift stopped, the doors opened and I saw a firefighter standing in front of me. He helped me to my feet and asked me if I had seen anymore survivors. I shook my head and said, "No." He helped me to where the front desk used to be, then stopped. I looked back at him, but there was no trace of him. Replacing him was a 6 foot wall. I looked back up towards the blocked passage way and saw a hole big enough for me to fit through.

I worked my way towards the hole and got on my hands and knees. I took off my heels, put them in my hands, and started crawling. When I got maybe halfway through the hole, I heard a crash. I knew this place was falling apart and I tried to keep the tears back. And I kept moving on. I finally got out and an officer was standing right in front of me like the firefighter. I gathered myself together and the officer helped me to an ambulance. I reached in my purse and pulled out my phone. As I dialed Sam's phone number, I was praying she was alright. When the number dialed, I waited for a couple of seconds when I heard a voice. Thankfully, it was Sam's.

She said she had a giant wound, but was coming out soon. I hung up and set my phone in my lap. About five minutes later, Sam came out of the other tower doors propped up against a firefighter. She was put on a stretcher and put in an ambulance. I hope she was okay, and I'm glad I'm alive. Later that day, I went to the hospital and visited Sam. She was alive and stable and I was glad. I hoped she would be leaving soon and she was.

You've heard my story now and you know how I felt. I was traumatized and that memory will be with me forever. I now have a job as a cook and when I tell this story to my customers, they listen. Whenever I tell this story, people listen. Humanity will never be the same after this event, and people will never forget what happened on September 11, 2001.

Cazia Nelson

CHAPTER 22

2001
The Stolen Treasure from 9/11

By: Cazia Amy Nelson

"Don't Worry Be Happy" is the song I sang as I ate my joyful breakfast.   A typical Tuesday but that Tuesday was special.   My mom was finally getting a promotion, an increase of $20 a day.   She works at the World Trade Center in the Twin Towers.   This is my home the Big Apple, New York City.   My mom slammed the door in a rush like every day, yep regularly, mom is late again.   By the way my name is Nelson, Nelson Carter.

I watched TV at 8:00, my show was on, like any other Tuesday, but something felt wrong.   My show got cut off in the middle of the commercials at 8:45 am, by breaking news.   I take a large "gulp" and paid close attention. "The North Twin tower has been hit by a plane" The news reporter said.   My thoughts immediately reflected on my mom, she had been on the 80th floor for her promotion celebration, that's where the plane hit. I sobbed wildly, would she ever return.

I knew I had to act fast over my tears I ran to the phone to call my dad; my parents had been divorced for quite some time now. All I heard over my tears was "This number no longer exist, good bye." I called my dad's closest friend, Mr. Banker. He answered and told me the worst news. My father is dead. "He had acted crazy from his problems and somebody shot him endlessly" Mr. Banker said. I dropped the phone and sprinted as fast as I can to my grandparents' house, with everything I can hold. "I guess this is my home now." I said as I approached the steps.

Sitting by my window every night I remember my mom. But my grandma makes me feel better; she told me the sweetest bedtime stories. They often made me laugh. Finally Grandpa left and I could watch TV. I can finally watch news; maybe one of the found survivors is my mom. "Oh my gosh" Is all I can think. "There is a survivor found barely hurt. She is white with blonde hair, with brown eyes. Her initials are R.C.". All I could think was "Mom your still alive?" To find out I quickly grab money, for a bus, and set off to find my mom anywhere, anywhere at all.

I found a place to sleep and lie that my mom is on the way. Trying to sleep I ponder how to survive alone, a job is all I can think of. I will wake up to get a quick job.

I set off to find my mom after I got my $40. I pass the movie studio, walking my slowest. I couldn't help but notice I see a woman I recognize. I ran to the place and meet face to face with the recognizable woman. I curiously say "Mom is that you". She suddenly turns around and carries me out quickly. "Look doesn't be mad it's not what

120

it looks like". I ran away with tears of betrayal pouring out thinking "She is the most terrible person in the world." Though inside me feel there is a reason, I just can't.

"Nelson, wait let me explain!" I hear my mom holler running up to my room. I sit abruptly to everything that she says. She explains to me that it was just for money to take care of me. I give her a long bear hug, as she sings "Don't Worry be Happy".

Wedding music plays as my mom and new dad get married. I thought this day would never come, I guess our family is just blessed. We are a regular family, with a story now. Our new last name is the Carvers. Now we have just regular days, especially Tuesdays.

I love this book!

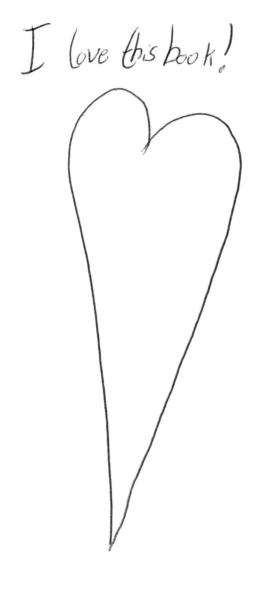

9 781941 247051